THE
INVISIBLE HAND

Life Story

Azima Melita Kolin

Matador
Unit E2 Airfield Business Park,
Harrison Road, Market Harborough,
Leicestershire. LE16 7UL
Tel: 0116 2792299
Email: books@troubador.co.uk
Web: www.troubador.co.uk/matador
Twitter: @matadorbooks

ISBN 978 1 8031 3035 4

British Library Cataloguing in Publication Data.
A catalogue record for this book is available from the British Library.

Printed and bound in the UK by TJ Books LTD, Padstow, Cornwall
Typeset in 11pt Adobe Garamond Pro by Troubador Publishing Ltd, Leicester, UK

Matador is an imprint of Troubador Publishing Ltd

To Rumi

Contents

Foreword

Have you ever looked back over your shoulder and sensed an invisible hand guiding your way? Whether you've lived eight decades, as Azima Melita has, or only a couple, whether you've had extraordinary adventures, as she has, or live a more circumscribed existence, whether you believe in a higher power or reject any kind of formal faith, traces of synchronicity and the touch of a meaningful design are hard to deny. At each significant threshold, you somehow knew which way to turn, and turning that way changed everything.

In this beautifully written life story, Azima Melita Kolin silently acknowledges a sacred something that leads her from an oppressive existence behind the Iron Curtain to an illustrious career as a concert pianist in Italy and Switzerland, where she studies with some of the great masters of the twentieth century who each recognise in her a talent she could never seem to acknowledge in herself. The Invisible Hand leads her to meet and marry a Scottish chieftain and move with him into his family's castle on the Isle of Skye where she co-founds a music festival and raises a family. But it also holds the dissolution of her marriage and the ensuing dissolution of her identity, yielding a state of no-self to which mystics of all traditions aspire. This is the moment when Azima Melita is led to the wisdom of the medieval Persian Sufi, Mevlana Jalaludin Rumi, who sweeps her into his metaphysical arms and engages her in a dance of classical music and poetry that unfolds for decades. The Invisible Hand also welcomes her to the desert for prolonged, star-studded, deeply quiet interludes where she rests in vast emptiness and discovers it to be overflowing with vibrant life.

And the Invisible Hand led her to me. Or the Hand that guides me led me to her. It doesn't matter. Our meeting has been one of the great blessings of my life. It was January 2004. Azima Melita had stumbled upon my translation of *Dark Night of the Soul*, by the sixteenth century Spanish mystic, John of the Cross, which led her to my translation of *The Interior Castle* by Teresa of Avila. These texts, transcending religiosity and pointing to a more universal heart-truth, deeply resonated with her. She wondered if I was a Sufi. She reached out. 'I have never done this before,' she wrote in the email she sent through my publisher, 'but when you mentioned that the relationship between Teresa of Avila and John of the Cross was like that of Rumi and Shams, I shivered, as if I was reading my own thoughts in your words.' When I enquired more about her, Azima told me she had recently translated (together with a Farsi speaker) a book of Rumi's poems called *Hidden Music*. The very same book, richly illustrated with Azima's paintings, was beside my bed, having been gifted to my husband and me as a wedding present. The Invisible Hand was parting the veil to show us that we were sisters in Spirit, and thus commenced a friendship that has spanned two decades and two continents.

In *Wild Mercy*, I wrote about Azima Melita as that rare being who excels in multiple art forms - music, poetry, painting - all of which are expressions of Divine Spirit. As the story of her life began to unfold over the course of our friendship, I encouraged her to write about it and she has sent me drafts of the evolving chapters over the last dozen years or so. I relished each fresh piece that arrived in my inbox. Not only were her adventures astounding and the cast of characters that populated her world highly intriguing, but her style was utterly charming. It had something to do with the fact that her first language is Bulgarian, not English, and so her syntax was quirky and delicious. She also has a straightforward way of painting a verbal picture that allows the story to take vibrant shape in the reader's mind.

The version you hold here is a distilled elixir of hundreds of pages of experiences and revelations Azima Melita originally documented. If no longer the unfiltered narrative I had the privilege of witnessing, this final edition offers us an immensely readable, touching memoir. And, more than that, it pays homage to the ferocious and loving Hand that guides and blesses every life.

Mirabai Starr

New Mexico, April 2021

BULGARIA

O n a warm afternoon in June a few years ago, I was sitting outside a café on the main square in Sofia when the words of a poem by Rumi came to me.

'All day I think about it and at night I say it –
where did I come from and what am I supposed to be doing?'

Yes, where did I come from? Facing the King's Palace, which, after the change of regime was turned into a National Gallery, I suddenly realised that the café was on the exact spot where the mausoleum of our president Georgi Dimitrov once stood. Every year, we were taken from school to pay our respects to the father of communism. People queued to see his corpse placed behind glass, on a black velvet bed, dressed in a black suit with a red rose on his chest. The dim, macabre light inside always made me shiver. On the way to my piano lessons as a young girl, I would detour along other streets, going out of my way to avoid the mausoleum. It affected the atmosphere of the whole town. Even the air around it smelled of death and decay. I loathed it.

Now the square was cheerful, filled with people sitting under umbrellas outside the cafes, eating, drinking and laughing. Children ran around, musicians were playing, artists painted pictures on the pavement. The grey, crumbling buildings I remembered, were carefully restored with adornments and figures on the facades I had never noticed before. They had once been private residences but were confiscated under communism. Now they were turned into banks and offices with imposing glass doors. Hearing Bulgarian spoken around me seemed odd; living abroad for so many years I felt a stranger in my native town. Everything seemed familiar yet altered beyond recognition. Sitting there trying to reconcile the past and present, my whole life suddenly appeared in front of my mind's eye as if in a film. I saw myself as the child in Sofia, student in Rome and Geneva, mother with two children on a remote Scottish island, artist in London. I had the overwhelming sense that some invisible force had compelled me in these different directions.

I left the café and walked the streets as if in a dream and found myself in front of the main concert hall, which looked dusty and neglected. Clearly, it had not been part of the city plans for improvement. I stood before the entrance that was once the hub of my student days, remembering how we hurried through the same door, excited and eager to hear the great soloists Richter, Gieseking, Gilels, Oistrakh, as well as many celebrated conductors. We were fortunate to hear Shostakovich symphonies premiered in his very presence, thanks to the courage and dedication of Konstantin Iliev, our principal conductor at the time. I could also see myself going through the artists' entrance, terrified, before playing a concerto with the orchestra, my hands frozen and trembling. The apartment of my best friend Christina was just opposite the back entrance, where before the concerts I used to go to calm my nerves and warm my hands in a bowl of water which her grandmother had heated for me. The building was still there. I stood for a long time looking at the windows of the apartment. Should I ring the bell? Would my old friend open the door and invite me in? I so wanted to see her sweet face appear, but the windows looked at me with empty and indifferent eyes. The people I loved are long gone. I continued on my walk. Every street and every corner mixed memory with loss. The Hungarian restaurant with red velvet seats and gipsy musicians where we used to eat goulash and drink heady wine after concerts was now a fast-food restaurant. The theatres looked unchanged, though now boutiques with fashionable clothes had sprung in between and smart shops were selling anything you could wish for, even pistols and rifles. Yet I could see old people rummaging through rubbish bins for scraps of food: beggars were on the streets. Freedom, without a doubt, had made everything more possible, but it had not improved the lives of my friends who stayed on.

The town had expanded hugely. Instead of little houses with gardens, a forest of high blocks had risen, obscuring the view of Vitosha mountain – the main attraction of the city. While living abroad, I used to have a dream; searching for my house in Sofia, getting lost, unable to recognise the town, similar to how I felt now. Another dream I remember was finding a gothic cathedral in the centre of town and being astonished as to why it was there. Then a gargoyle's hand beckoned me to the entrance. I went inside, surprised to see that it was not a church but a bar. There were bottles of whisky and all sorts of alcoholic drinks at the altar under the crucifix. I looked at Christ, and he winked at me. I now begin to understand that dream. Life is a joke. Communism ended in Bulgaria in 1989. On arrival at the airport after this date even the air felt different. Instead of heaviness and gloom, you could now breathe freely. What was I doing here? Maybe I had to come back to meet myself.

I didn't come here of my own accord and I can't leave that way.
Whoever brought me here will have to take me home.

Rumi

CHILDHOOD

I was born one hot August day at a most inconvenient time and place. And, though my mother used to tell me 'Coming out of the clinic with you felt as if I was carrying the sun in my arms', my birth cast a shadow on their future and ruined their plans to settle in Yugoslavia where my father, a doctor, was working. My mother, already pregnant, had gone back to Bulgaria to visit her family and suddenly the borders were closed, so I was born in Sofia. To his great disappointment, my father missed not only the birth of his daughter, but also the dream of a new country for his family. We remained stuck behind the Iron Curtain. It was war time. One vivid memory is being in my mother's arms as she is running in panic seeking shelter. I see the sky is full of terrifying black things.

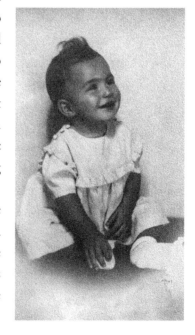

The first six years of my childhood were spent in Burgas, a port town on the Black Sea where my father returned to work. Here, life was still unaffected by the menacing clouds of communism gathering over the rest of the country.

Mother and Father

I remember going with my father to see the big ships moving in and out of the port, the people strolling around, laughing and chatting. There were still horse-carriages. I loved the clip-clop sound they made on the pavement, the shiny bells and colourful pompoms on the horses' necks. I so wanted to stroke the horses and would run after them much to my mother's horror. And the sea – I could never have enough of it. Sitting in the water, I was so absorbed by the patterns the waves left on the black sand that I never heard my mother's more and more urgent calls. I would not move and had to be carried, screaming and kicking, away from the beach to lunch and the dreaded afternoon siesta. I would sulk all the way home. But after the siesta, washed and dressed, my unruly hair wetted and combed, everything was happy again as I went with my parents, as everyone did, to stroll along the main street. *Shoes... so many feet in shoes and sandals; red, green, white... a forest of legs shuffling, stopping, moving. And voices... soft, loud, rising and falling like waves over my head: 'How lovely to see you... Oh, hasn't she grown!'*

How I wished they would stop talking so we could get to the stall with the green and yellow glass jars and have my promised ice cream. Once I held it in my hand, even though it dripped down my dress, I didn't mind anymore to whom they talked or for how long. The walk continued to the end of the main street and into a garden above the sea. This was the scary bit. After the brightly lit street full of people and noise, here it was dark and cool. Holding tight onto my father's hand, I would listen to the roar of the sea in the darkness, and stare at the white-crested waves rolling towards me like crocodile's teeth ready to gobble me up, both frightened and transfixed. Even now, as I write, the salty smell of the sea mixed with the sweet scent of petunias and grilled fish from a stall beneath the garden, fills my nostrils.

Smell brings vivid memories – the smell of warm earth or freshly baked bread. I used to tear off bits of the crust under the disapproving glance of my mother. As people did not have ovens in their houses, everybody carried their lunch on trays to the bakery. I was frightened of the baker, towering above the crowd in his stained apron and bare shoulders, throwing the trays with a long wooden shovel into the black mouth of the oven. He looked like a fiery monster. But the aroma coming out of the bakery at noon when collecting our lunch was overwhelming. I would watch a succession of dishes coming out – meats with golden potatoes, chickens with vegetables, cakes. My nose trailed after them – other peoples' always seemed more tempting than ours. Smell conveys more than words. I could even smell if my mother was angry or my father in a bad mood. No wonder they used to called me *Kutcho,* which in Bulgarian means dog. Maybe in another life that is what I was.

Sound also had a strange power over me. One evening in the scary bit of the sea garden, I heard strange noises. I asked my father what it was. Somebody, he told me, was playing a piano. We followed the sound down the stairs to a white building near the beach and walked into a big hall where people were dancing. On a brightly lit platform was a black man in a white suit stroking a big black animal with black and white teeth making the most incredible sound. I could not take my eyes off his fingers. If my fingers were the same colour, I decided, I would be able to play like him. Can I touch his hands? I asked my father. He walked me to the front and whispered something to the pianist. With a big smile the man lifted me up on the stage and sat me on the stool next to him: 'Here, little one, now I will play something specially for you!' My eyes were fixed on his hands. When he finished, he shook my hand and lowered me into my father's arms. I checked my hand immediately, but it looked the same as before. I kept examining my hands all the way home, and stubbornly refused to wash them before going to bed. Maybe tomorrow, when I wake up, they will be the same colour as his. They were not, but on that memorable evening the seed of a pianist was planted.

Being an only child, my parents took me along everywhere they went, often to parties with friends. I remember being left on a sofa watching the hands of the clock move slowly and being lulled to sleep by the sound of clinking glasses and singing. My parents would wake me late at night and, holding their hands, I would sleepwalk home. We lived in an apartment on the second floor of a house which my parents rented from a Jewish couple who had no children themselves, so I was always alone, playing with make-believe friends on the roof terrace.

I met my first friend when I was three. He was an old man who sold cigarettes and newspapers from a little kiosk in front of the house. My mother often exchanged a few words with him as we came home. The kiosk with its small window seemed a magic world for me. Curious to see what was inside, I nagged my mother until one day (she must have asked him), the door opened, and he invited me in. I was captivated by the things on the shelves of his tiny house – boxes, jars with sweets, bottles, matches, and by the smell of tobacco and paper; things I had not encountered before. He gave me a sweet and made a space on his chair. From then on, every morning I knocked on his door and would sit next to him. 'Good morning, little helper. Are you ready?' he would ask, giving me a sweet out of a box kept especially for me. He would then let me hand out the newspapers to the customers. I chatted non-stop. He listened and smiled. Looking out from inside the dark kiosk, seeing people walking on the street and smiling at me when I handed the newspapers, made me feel very important and grown up.

One spring day, I must have been five at the time, I was playing with my dolls on the floor, while my mother was bent over a sewing machine, frowning and struggling with a piece of material she had cut from a curtain. Something was up. I hovered around her asking questions. 'Go away. Can't you see I am busy? Go and play elsewhere if you want to have a new dress for tomorrow.' Dress for tomorrow? Why? I kept asking. 'I will tell you if you promise to leave me in peace.' I promised. 'Tomorrow your father is taking you to see the hospital where he works. There you can play with children in the garden. So, be good and let me finish your dress.'

This was too much. A new dress, going in a horse carriage, playmates, I could hardly sleep that night. In the morning, climbing into the carriage next to my father with my new dress on, I felt like a princess: no one could have been happier on that sunny day. The pompoms danced on the horse's neck, puffy clouds raced in the sky and I waved proudly at people walking on the street. I was in heaven. Arriving at the hospital, I saw a dozen children chasing each other around a disused fountain full of greenish water. My father left me with them and went inside. It was such fun to have *real* playmates. I ran like mad around the garden with them, we splashed water over each other, we climbed on the rim of the fountain and jumped off again and again when suddenly, everything went quiet. In the semi-darkness, black things were swimming in front of my eyes in slow motion. Time stopped in this strange silent world… Then, I felt myself pulled out, held upside down in the air, like a fish, terrified and blinded by the sunlight. My father was frantically ripping my dress to pieces until, I found myself naked and shivering in front of a crowd of doctors, nurses and children. I was wrapped in hospital towels like a parcel and taken home. My father must have been panic-stricken to find me floating face down in the water. If the children had not called out for help, I would have drowned, but tearing my dress in front of everyone left a big scar. Being joyous became a bad omen, a warning for disaster. The fear of joy is characteristic of the Slavic temperament. My grandmother was a perfect example: the moment she saw me happy, she would start spitting in all directions and crossing herself, in case the devil took me.

One afternoon my parents interrupted the game I was playing, insisting I should go to bed at once. It was urgent, they said, and I had no choice. I threw a big tantrum. 'Why? It is not dark yet, I won't go to bed, I won't go!' 'Listen, be a good girl and go to bed now. If you do, tomorrow morning you will find a doll by your bed that can talk. But now you must go to bed!' I held onto a chair and wouldn't let go. All threats and promises failed until they mentioned strawberry jam. This was something precious and rare. A grateful patient had given my father a pot which lived on the top of a cupboard out of my reach. No matter how hard I pleaded, I was not allowed to have any; it was only for very special occasions. Now, they told me, I could eat the whole pot if I went to bed.

My brother was born that night, delivered by my father. In the morning, as soon as I opened my eyes, I looked for the promised doll beside my bed but there was nothing. Sobbing, I ran to their room: 'Look here,' they beamed,

Mother and brother

'this is your little brother.' What kind of doll was this? The red, wrinkled face peeping out of the blanket didn't look anything like a doll, and it didn't talk either. I felt cheated. If this was the promised doll, I didn't want it. 'Be patient. Your brother will grow and, one day you will have a friend for life.' But I was inconsolable. So, what if I had the strawberry jam? The tears rolling down my cheeks made it taste salty. I felt betrayed and lonelier than before. At first, my little brother slept a lot. He looked pretty harmless in his cot, but soon his piercing cries made him impossible to ignore, so I retreated to the roof terrace with my imaginary friends. From time to time, I would check on him, but he wasn't the playmate I so wanted. He slept, he cried, he ate – it was all he did. As the months went by, his face filled up, his little hands and feet moved up and down into the air, he even began to look cute, but still, he was not a playmate. Once, left alone with him, I leaned over and whispered eagerly in his ear: 'Come on, grow faster!' He ignored me and kept kicking the air. I repeated the same a bit louder, and again, even louder, until his face contracted into a frown and then into an ear-splitting yell that brought my mother running into the room. 'What have you done to him you stupid girl?' I got a smack and joined in the crying. Life was unjust. 'You are big now and must know what to do or not to do,' my mother would say. 'He is small, and you must look after him.' I had to wait a long time before I realised how wonderful it was to have a brother.

SOFIA

I was six when my father decided to move the family to Sofia for the sake of our education. I can't remember how we got there, but felt myself falling into a dark hole, deeper and deeper. I couldn't understand why we had to leave our sunny home by the sea to live squashed in one room in a spooky and dark house. Tall birch trees obscured the windows and the greenish light that trickled through the leaves made the room even gloomier. We shared the second floor of this house with my father's sister from Argentina. She had come with her two teenage boys to visit her mother but had been unable to return due to the war. While waiting for permission to leave, she had offered us a room to help settle in Sofia. The papers did not come for a long time, so she was living in one room with her sons and our family in the other. It made life difficult for everybody.

Our room was a sitting room and bedroom all in one. In the day, the beds were transformed into sofas and the dining table was used for our homework. The entrance hall was dark, the bathroom even darker, and the kitchen the most depressing place of all. Narrow and north facing, it had one mouldy cupboard, a wobbly wooden table and an iron stove in the corner, black as a coffin and almost always cold. Wood and coal were in short supply. In winter, going to the kitchen was like stepping into a freezer. It took a long time to get the stove going before my mother could cook a meal. How they managed to feed us in these times is hard to imagine. Food was scarce and one had to queue not only for

In Sofia with mother

bread but for everything else as well. I still remember my mother's desperate face when she came back empty-handed after queuing for hours. No wonder if, in that cramped kitchen, clashes between my mother and my aunt erupted daily.

The kitchen balcony looked into a backyard, littered with fragments of china, glass, skeletons of prams, piles of rubbish and broken objects: leftovers of lives shattered by the war still lingering in the rubble. And now we had Stalin's regime of terror. Fear and paranoia reigned over the country. Everyone dreaded being put on the blacklist as an enemy of socialism. No one could be trusted. People disappeared without trace. Women would hide themselves under dark coats and scarves, afraid to wear lipstick in case they were accused of belonging to the bourgeoisie. Unless one's parents were partisans, peasants or factory workers it wasn't safe. As no one in my family fitted these categories, the future looked bleak.

I wasn't aware of all this at the time, but I could smell fear and despair around and it made me miserable. I didn't dare to ask why everybody looked so downcast and angry. My mother became irritable: the gentle face I was used to, no longer there. My father looked so gloomy and cross that I became frightened of him. One night I was woken by angry voices: mother and father shouting at each other. I sat in my bed but could not utter a sound to warn them that I was awake. I hid under the covers but could still hear them. I felt guilty. This was something I wasn't supposed to hear: my parents were at war. My trust was shattered. I could never tell them that I had heard this terrible fight and felt totally alone and forsaken. That night, I orphaned myself.

In the backyard, which was a bomb site, a group of girls would often play. Day after day, glued to the window, I watched them skipping with a rope, longing to join them but lacking the courage to do so. Weeks passed before I made my first attempt, but their unfriendly *don't you dare* glances sent me running home in tears. I was not accepted in their circle. Tired of looking at my sulking, *nobody wants to play with me* face, mother decided to take the matter in hand. 'Come on, enough is enough. I can't bear seeing you like this anymore. We will walk the street together and find you a friend.' She gave me a slice of bread topped with sugar, took my hand, and we walked in the neighbourhood in search of children, my mother peeping over the garden fences. Soon she spotted two girls pushing a small boy on a swing. She went up to one of the girls about my age and spoke to her. Before I knew it, they'd put me on the swing, which all three children then pushed. Up and down I went, trees and sky, faces and houses, all swung past until I felt dizzy and asked them to let me down. Meanwhile, my mother had slipped away without me noticing. Standing unsteadily on the ground, I noticed one of the girls smiling at me shyly. I asked her name. 'Violeta' she replied. Violeta. I liked the name and her shiny black hair. I liked her a lot. From then on, we became inseparable. We would walk to school together, giggling and watching out for black cats crossing the road. These brought terrible bad luck. After school we often played at her house with her little sister, her brother and Volga their tabby cat. It was so lively and cheerful, I wanted to stay and never return home.

PIANO AND REBELLION

A couple of years later, playing catch in the ruins, I hid in the doorway of a little house across our yard. I then heard a furious scratching at the door, and a dog started barking wildly. I was terrified. The door opened and I fell into the arms of a woman. 'Don't be frightened, my dear.' The woman took my hand in hers and patted the dog's head. 'See, she is harmless. Her name is Stella. If you want to play with her, just ring the bell. By the way, my name is Dora.' How kind she was! When there was nobody to play with in the courtyard, I would knock at her door and ask to play with Stella. She always let me in with a smile. When the dog had enough, it fell asleep on her lap, and she and I talked together. Nobody at home had time to hear me, so I was enchanted to have such a patient and attentive listener. Soon my visits became a regular thing.

One day she had a visitor and asked me to wait in the hallway. I noticed a door and being curious, opened it and went inside. The curtains were drawn, letting only a faint light through. I bumped into a chair, but gradually got used to the dark and when I did, saw a piano in the corner. I opened the lid and touched the keys gently, then shut it immediately, afraid to be found where I shouldn't be. But I couldn't resist for long and opening the lid again I pressed a bit harder on the keys. The sounds had a magical effect. I continued up and down the keyboard, listening as they came out, waiting until they vanished, so absorbed that I forgot to leave the room. Far from being angry Dora said I could play as much as I liked. The piano drew me like a magnet. Every day I ran straight there. I would sit on the stool, bend my body right down until my ear was under the keyboard, then lift my arm above the keyboard, strike a note with one finger and listen to the vibrations until they faded into nothing. Then strike another, and another. The vibrations transported me to a magical world of columns shimmering in the air. I wish I could wave a wand now and hear, with the same unspoilt ear as then, these sounds that once enveloped me like a gentle hand holding all things.

I wanted a piano. I asked my father to get me one. He looked shocked by my request. 'Really? Are you sure?' Yes, I was sure. There was nothing I desired as much. But then, nothing happened. I kept begging, and my father would wave his hand impatiently. 'Stop it. We've had this conversation already.' Eventually, I gave up asking. Then one day, when I least expected it, a black upright piano appeared with Bechstein written in gold letters. I couldn't believe my eyes. I jumped up to my father like a mad dog, kissing him, thanking him wildly, and stroked the shiny lid and the ivory keys.

How did he manage to find a brand-new piano when even bread was difficult to get? There were no shops for musical instruments. It turned out a Jewish patient of his had imported a piano for his son, who refused to go anywhere near it, so he was selling it again. That my father happened to be there at that moment was lucky, but when he told me, years later, that he also disliked the piano, it was even more astonishing that he got it for me.

The piano changed my life and everybody else's in the house. For a start it made the room even smaller. After the initial excitement, it became clear I needed a piano teacher. At first, my parents asked a friend of theirs to teach me. I disliked her from the start. She forbade my usual position under the keyboard, sat me upright, curled my fingers over the keys, and exhausted me with threatening commands: 'Keep your back straight. Do not flatten your fingers. Keep the rhythm, play with one hand first, now the two together…!' The lessons became a torture. Gone were the magical sounds I loved so much. I resented having to practice after school instead of playing with my friends.

Beware of what you want, as you might get it. So, the saying goes. Now I had my piano, it weighed on me like a huge black monster. If only I could escape but my father was firm as a rock. 'You wanted a piano, so now you must practice.' I was unaware at the time of the sacrifice my parents had made. Every night after we went to bed, they translated medical books from German to Bulgarian, to pay for the piano. This went on for many years. I was caught and had to fulfil my end of the bargain. My father, like a prison guard, sat in his armchair next to me as I practiced. He would often doze off, but if I tried to sneak away, he would wake up. So, I devised a system: spinning on the rotating stool, I would hit one key *en passant* and another on return, thus keeping him asleep by the constant sound, but it was such a waste of time. The days followed each other with stifling regularity: school, homework, practice, piano lessons. I hated both my teacher and my father and prayed to God they might die.

Then, one day Dimo Goncharov, a friend of my mother and well-known conductor of the Opera choir, came into the room, beaming and light as a feather. 'Well, my dear, come, we will play a game. Can you guess what it is?' I looked at him surprised. 'Don't worry, I am sure you will like it. It's called the piano game! 'A game? I lit up. 'But I want to make one thing clear first. I don't want you to practice for more than fifteen minutes, and only if you feel like it!' His words felt like balm to my ears. 'Yes, you heard right, only fifteen. If you feel bored, you must stop and do something else. Then, you can come back, but remember, the most important thing is to have fun!' My resistance melted. He would put an apple on one side of the piano, and each time I repeated a phrase, he asked me to move it to the other side.

Dimo

Every lesson he invented a different game; I played for rabbits, birds and dogs that he painted on pieces of paper, or for sweets which I was allowed to eat after repeating a phrase ten times. Soon, the props became redundant. I ran straight to the piano after school, doubling the prescribed fifteen minutes, eager to please him. I could hardly wait for the day of my lesson. I fell in love with him and the piano. His son, a few years younger than me, was also learning, and he often gave us lessons together in their home. When we progressed enough to play a piece of music, he told us: 'You must both learn to play in public right from the start, so I've invited a few friends to listen to you and, after, we will have cakes and games.'

That Sunday, chairs were arranged around the piano, the table was set with biscuits and a cake and my mother curled my hair for the occasion. I was more excited showing my curls to others than playing for them. Dimo was brilliant at everything – reciting poems, telling stories, painting pictures, and playing cards tricks. The Sunday gatherings became a regular thing which I came to treasure. It was here I heard a poem recited for the first time and here I learned to draw. Always amusing and enthusiastic, his presence brightened everything.

Sometimes, our families spent the summer together by the sea. We swam and built sandcastles, but the greatest delight was listening to Dimo. 'Do you want to hear the sea telling its tale?' he would ask his son and me. Yes, yes, but how? 'Keep very still, shut your eyes and listen … listen to the waves, coming and going. Can you hear the silence between them?' We would listen with ears pressed on the sand. 'You must be very still and listen, because the sea can only whisper.' We listened. 'Wow', he would say, 'I'm just beginning to hear it, can you?' It didn't matter if we did or not, just trying to hear the sea whispering was thrilling. Then came the birds. 'Now, lie on the sand and look at the seagulls flying in the sky. Follow them as far as you can with your eyes. I will tell you a secret – if you keep on looking without blinking, soon you will feel your wings grow… can you feel them? One day you too will be able to fly like them!' Everything seemed possible with him. Life was a fairy-tale. He was a master, who taught without teaching.

One day I was waiting for my lesson, impatient to show him how well I could play a minuet by Mozart, but he did not come. 'Go out and play with your friends, my mother said, I will call you when he comes.' But she never did. When I came back, she looked troubled and kept her face down. 'What happened?' I asked. She took me in her arms, unable to speak. 'I don't know how to tell you. Something terrible has happened …' She was sobbing and I too began to cry. 'Dimo died.' I was thunderstruck. 'It's not true,' I shouted. No, no, it is impossible; he is not dead! Not him…' I cried. We both cried until numb. I felt as if I had died with him.

Two days later, we went to the opera house where his body was laid on a black podium covered with flowers. Beethoven's funeral march sounded in the hall. Crowds of people walked around the open coffin in step with the music, to pay their last respects and kiss him goodbye. When I approached the coffin, my heart was beating so wildly that I felt it would burst out of my chest. I kissed his cheek, cold as a stone. My world had shattered. He was no more. After the funeral, everything became grey and empty. My body went to school and back, but I was absent. I had no recollection of what went on in school or at home. Only a small part of me functioned. Phrases like *new teacher, entry exams,* reached me as if from another planet. Only my heart repeated with each beat … *He is gone, he is gone.* Without him, the world was hopeless and dull.

Daydreaming became my only refuge. There was a tree at school in front of the classroom window, which became the focus of my attention. I used to hang my worries on its branches and tell it all my troubles: how much I missed Dimo, how much I loathed school and the quarrels at home, how frightened I was of my father. The branches swaying in the wind seemed to answer and comfort me. I was sure the tree heard and understood me. Sometimes it became a tall cypress in a peaceful sunny garden by the sea, surrounded by little white houses. I could see it all so vividly. I could even smell cypresses in the air and hear laughter and music. Then with a shock I would find the teacher standing over me in the same dull classroom.

Going home was equally depressing. I used to walk very slowly, delaying my return for as long as possible. One day, passing by the main cathedral, I went inside and sat on a chair, watching the babushkas lighting candles, murmuring prayers and bowing in front of the icons. It felt very peaceful in the flickering candlelight. The faces of saints seemed to come towards me from the frescos on the walls. The scent of frankincense and beeswax lingering in the air had a calming effect. I felt safe. Sitting quietly one day, I was suddenly transported by the voices of the cathedral choir – it must have been during a service. My eyes filled with tears. I went at the same time the next day and the day after hoping to hear the voices again, but everything was silent. And yet, going there helped me to face my homework and piano practice. Luckily, my father was not as strict about my school results as he was about my piano.

In school, we sat at hard, wooden desks with our hands behind our backs as was the rule. Portraits of Lenin and Stalin looked down on us from the classroom wall as if to oversee the compulsory daily hour of positive-socialist-criticism. 'Now, class,' the teacher would say, 'we must be truthful and say who has behaved properly. We must get rid of all traces of the bourgeoisie in order to become worthy of wearing the red scarf of the pioneer. I invite you all to tell the class about your friends' behaviour and also what your parents talked about at home. Who will be the first to start?' Many hands rose eagerly. Rosa said: 'Ivan hit Maria yesterday, and she cried like a baby. This is not how a real pioneer should behave.' Olga said, 'Yana did not answer when I asked her how to spell a word. She did not behave like a proper friend.' Then Chavdar fell into the trap. 'My mother said that before socialism the shops were full of food.' This put his parents straight on the blacklist. We had to stand at the blackboard one by one, listen to the criticism, apologise, and promise to do better. We, the pioneers, the builders of socialism, were encouraged to tell on our friends and family, to spy and compete in order to gain points and please our benevolent father Stalin.

Every day, mother would give the usual warning at the door: 'You must never speak in school about what you hear at home.' 'I know. Don't worry I won't say a thing.' 'But you understand why, don't you? Not a word, or you will be left without parents. Is that clear?' It was still dark as I left home in the long winters. I would go down the stairs, my mother repeating *never tell a word*, and out into the freezing fog. It had an unpleasant sickly-yellow tinge in the dim streetlight. The fear that hung over the whole town was the same sickly yellow colour and never lifted.

Feeling miserable, unhappy at home and in school, a wild idea came to me. I planned it without telling anyone, not even my best friend, Violeta. I took a small piece of paper and wrote. LONG LIVE CHURCHILL. I had no idea who Churchill was, but had heard his name mentioned in school as an enemy of the communist regime. To cover my tracks, I carefully slanted the letters to the left, folded the piece of paper, put it in the drawer under my desk and lifted my hand: 'Comrade, look what I found under my desk.'

The teacher took the piece of paper, read it, and all hell broke out. We were not allowed to leave school and the interrogations then began. First, everybody in my class had to write a sentence on a piece of paper, then the whole school. The papers were examined by handwriting experts and compared with the paper I presented. Government officials and militia walked from class to class, like hunting dogs sniffing around, determined to find the culprit. I watched, terrified, wondering what might happen to my parents if I was discovered, but tried to look normal and calm throughout the ordeal. It lasted an interminable week. To my immense relief, they failed to discover the culprit and the search was abandoned. I was triumphant but it was a lucky escape. I dare not think what would had happened if I had been found out. I never told a soul about this and my parents died not knowing my terrible secret.

BACH AND BOOKS

When my mother presented me to my new piano teacher, Lily Chenkova, I refused to shake hands and looked away, hardly acknowledging her presence. I was still mourning my beloved Dimo. A week later, I found myself in front of her apartment. I rang the bell, secretly determined to resist her in every possible way. When she opened the door, I took a step back alarmed by the enormous teeth protruding from her mouth. She pointed at a chair in the entrance hall. 'Sit here and take your shoes off. No shoes in my house.' Walking in my socks into the room was like slipping on ice, her parquet floor was so polished. She sat me on the sofa, took my hands and examined them carefully. 'You have good hands for the piano but …' She left the room and coming back with a pair of scissors, proceeded to cut my nails right to the skin before sitting me at the piano. 'Oh dear, I can see that you have been badly taught. We'll have to change your position. You must forget all you have learned up to now and work hard if you want to pass the entry exam. We haven't got much time, so listen carefully and do as I say. Is that clear?'

I walked home fuming, stamping my feet on the pavement – *I hate you, horrible, ugly witch…* That's how I entered the next stage of my musical career – angry, shoeless, short-nailed, burdened with new finger positions and a long list of pieces to learn. Competition to enter the Music School was fierce, and I had to pass the exam, otherwise, my parents kept repeating, there was no future. Lily would ring my father when I got home from the lesson. Seeing his face darken like a storm cloud, my stomach would tighten, waiting for his anger to rain down on my head. 'She says you are not concentrating. You must work harder to pass the exam. Your future depends on it.' Much as I resented Lily Chenkova, she proved to be an excellent teacher and after two years, to my parents' great relief and mine, I passed the exam and enrolled at the music school in Sofia. Though the pressure was off, the joy of music I had experienced with Dimo was gone. For a couple of years, I continued to drag myself to lessons, tired and bored.

One day as I was waiting my turn, the girl before me played a Three Part Invention by Bach and suddenly my ears opened. I not only heard but saw the three voices moving and dancing in the room. The first one took a step, the second joined, and then the third. The voices mingled, paused for a moment, ran in opposite directions, and came together again. I felt as if was inside the music, moving with the melody, stunned and enchanted. Walking home that day, the streets, the people, the whole town looked bright and cheerful, as if a door had opened to a new sunlit world. I was finally present. The grey had lifted and the world was filled with colour. The winter of absence was over.

Rumen

In the piano class there was a handsome boy called Rumen. We often walked together after lessons, grumbling about Lily and laughing over her terrible teeth. We would play our pieces to each other at my house, or I would visit his, where the living room had shelves filled with books by French, Russian, Spanish and German authors. My parents' house was also full of books, but these looked much more interesting. Leafing through the pages, I asked if I could borrow a few. 'Of course. Take as many as you like but bring them back. My father is very fussy about his collection.' The first books I took were Tolstoy's *Anna Karenina* and the short stories of Maupassant. Then there was no stopping me.

How powerful these first encounters are: first friendship, first novel, first love. I often went to borrow books from my friend's library, especially romantic novels, and inevitably fell hopelessly in love with the librarian. He was dating another girl, so I kept my feelings to myself, taking the role of a confidante instead. I suffered in silence, like a fictional heroine, and would even go with him on the way to their daily rendezvous, where he would wave me goodbye and I would walk on alone. There was a bench on which I used to sit, musing upon my fate, wallowing in self-pity which tasted pleasantly bittersweet. Being left out made me feel rather special. And so it went on: I would listen to Rumen's account of their relationship, flattered by his confidences and grateful for any crumbs of attention. Other friends also began to share their love stories and disappointments with me and I became popular as a consoler of the broken-hearted.

I still had Bach and my books. Inspired by an idea I must have read somewhere, I created a secret society. Every Thursday evening, I invited home a small gathering of friends to read poetry, passages from novels, and stories from the lives of musicians and artists. We would squeeze around a small table in my room, reading under the light of lampshade I had made out of green paper. I can't remember why green, but it felt very important at the time. At the end we would share any food we could find: a boiled egg, biscuits, sometimes even a piece of cake that a friend's mother had baked. Our animated discussions would continue long into the night. We moaned about the deprivations of the socialist regime – the lack of freedom. We fantasised about life in the West – images we had from pictures of fancy cars and smiling people in magazines and films that were circulating underground. Looking back now, I believe socialism did us a great favour. There were few outside attractions; no bars, no clubs, no money for drinks, no luxury shops (cinema was cheap but showed mostly Russian war films), so we had to create our own world. And it was a beautiful one – full of dreams, high ideals and a thirst for knowledge.

Theoretically, we were free to practice any religion but when my mother became a professor at the University, she could not be seen in church, or she would lose her job. For us church became a sanctuary all the more desirable for being suspect. Bach's sacred music was also banned, so we would copy it out by hand and sing it in secret. If we had had the distractions and freedoms of the West, I wonder if we would have read as much or spent our time discussing and playing music with such passion.

MUSIC SCHOOL

The Higher Music School was situated in a residential area reserved for embassies and government officials. Once a Catholic institution built by the Vatican at the beginning of the century, it had been confiscated by the communist government. Overlooking a garden, its large windows, marble stairs and oak-panelled walls retained something of their former glory even after years of neglect. Here we were taught all subjects except science, which was replaced by history of music, polyphony and composition. Because of the rigorous entrance exam, the classes were small, and we were under great pressure to achieve. When I think back to this time, I only remember the fun and boundless energy we had. A violinist in my class, whose enormous head seemed far too big for his body, would sit at the piano and play jazz during break. Soon, violins, cellos and trumpets joined in, while the rest of us danced on the top of the grand piano and on the desks. It was exhilarating. Inevitably, a teacher would burst into the room and send us to the Director. Jazz was considered decadent – we could be expelled from school for playing it. Luckily, the Director turned a deaf ear to the policy. He scolded us but always let us go. To keep watch on us, the Ministry of Culture sent a communist party member, an uneducated, provincial man whose only qualification was being a partisan during the war. Poor man, he had no idea what challenges lay waiting for him, having never heard of classical music in his life. We tore him to pieces, imitated his

Music school

dialect, made fun of him, asked questions about Bach or Beethoven and laughed uncontrollably at his ridiculous answers. Our aim was to humiliate him, and we made sure we succeeded. But he turned our cruel game on its head, becoming more knowledgeable about music that we could ever have imagined. He spent a whole year taking secret lessons in the history of music, learned to read music, attended hundreds of concerts and accumulated an impressive collection of records. What a lesson.

In our class was a horn player who managed to rid us of our hateful school uniform. He was rather fat and came up with an ingenious plan to borrow a uniform at least three sizes too small. Squeezing his bulk into it, the jacket split down the back, revealing naked flesh. His arms stuck out of the sleeves like tree branches in mid-air. However, the cherry on the top of the cake was a tiny hat on his bushy hair, tied with a red ribbon under the chin. He strutted through school like a stuffed scarecrow, waving his arms and bumping into the teachers, who were unable to stop him and couldn't manage to hide their smiles. Uniforms were dropped. We also rebelled against the obligatory Russian lessons, which, regrettably, resulted in my not speaking this beautiful language. Our teacher was an old man from Belarus, very short, humble, and frightened even of his own shadow. Remembering how relentlessly we teased him, fills me with shame. We would walk behind him, imitating his accent, or hide under his desk echoing his words. The poor man looked pathetic and on the verge of tears, but we giggled on until, trembling with rage, he sent us to the Director – exactly what we wanted, since once out of the classroom we escaped from school. Forming a single file, one leg on the curb and one on the road, we wobbled like ducks along the streets to the Cathedral, where a young priest we had befriended, told us the stories of the frescos on the walls. Here, for the first time, we learned about Jesus and his disciples and the thrill of escaping from a Russian lesson was heightened not only by the threat of expulsion from school but also by the fascinating stories we heard.

We pursued our musical careers with the support and encouragement, not only of our parents and teachers, but also of the communist regime. On one hand we had good teachers, educated in the European musical traditions, and on the other, we profited from the government's obsession with achievement. Culture was regarded as a showcase for the West, requiring excellent musicians, dancers, and athletes to win first prizes in international competitions. Every prize and medal won, glorified communism. As the slogan went – *Each victory is a nail in the coffin of capitalism.* Great artists like Richter, Oistrakh and Rostropovich were regarded as government property. The income from their tours abroad was taken by the State. Artists had to obey the rules of the party, otherwise they could not perform or publish their works. Dissident writers had to keep their manuscripts hidden, but still, their works secretly reached the bookshelves in the West.

Shostakovich was our hero. We never missed a concert of his music and were privileged to attend many premieres of his symphonies in Sofia where he was present. He used to sit on his own in the balcony above the orchestra, nervously wiping his spectacles with a white handkerchief. I will never forget his tortured face. Life under Stalin had left its mark. His music was officially denounced both in 1936 and 1948. Most of his works were banned, and he was forced to repent publicly. His music revealed more poignantly than any literary work I know, the horror, hopelessness and desolation during Stalin's regime. In it we found moral support, a kind of musical revenge, which voiced what nobody could express in words. We screamed at the top of our voices, *bravo, bravo* from the back of the hall, stamping our feet. After a long-standing ovation, we would spill out onto the street, exhilarated – then gather under a lamp post sharing the wonder. Then the militia would find us. 'Disperse at once! Or you will go to prison'.

We disliked Russians intensely. We saw them as repulsive replicas of Stalin. After all, it was he who authorised the Red Army to plunder and rob citizens of their possessions. Whole families were driven at gunpoint out of their homes and thousands vanished without a trace. Those who dared to protest were sent to Siberia. In the time of Stalin's terror, Russians became bogeymen with whom mothers frightened their children. Russian propaganda posters were everywhere. We loathed the Russians.

It was years later in the summer of 1966, that a different understanding came to me. I was with a group of students from the Music School, attending master classes at the Liszt Academy in Weimar. Delighted to be away from Bulgaria for the first time, we wandered through the cobbled streets of the old town, visiting the houses of Goethe and Schiller, Liszt and Mendelssohn, and going to concerts in the evenings. But our fun was soon interrupted by a visit from a Russian officer. We were to give a concert for a unit of the Russian army stationed nearby. An evening wasted on Russians! We had no choice. A few days later we were taken in a covered military truck to a secret location outside Weimar. Nothing could have prepared us for the astonishing vision when they unfastened the truck's cover. A sea of blue-eyed, blond-headed youths surrounded us, staring in awe. A mass of hands stretched up to lift us down from the truck, touching us, as if making sure we were real. Bodies pushed forward, forming a tight circle around us. They glanced nervously around to make sure there were no officers in sight, and then poured out a torrent of grievances. *'We have been stuck here for three years... we only get one letter a year from home... we are never allowed out in town... you are the first people from the outside world...'* Voices from all directions competed for our attention; faces glowed with excitement. Like a thousand-legged animal, the whole group, with us in the middle, moved to where the concert was to be held. At the sound of a whistle, they suddenly broke away, formed into lines and marched into the hall. We hardly had time to collect our instruments and scores before going on stage. I don't remember exactly what we played, something by Mozart, maybe some Bach, but the sight of those young soldiers packed like sardines, listening with their whole being, so still, so quiet that you could hear a pin drop, was unforgettable. At the end, they sprang to their feet as one, clapping, whistling, stamping in frenzy, until an officer barked a command, and they were marched back to the barracks. They blew kisses as they waved goodbye, but the light in their eyes had died. The spell was over. I still feel pity for those young boys.

We were ordered to follow the officers for refreshments. The dining room was shockingly bleak under naked light bulbs suspended from the ceiling. Seated, ill at ease, with an officer on each side, we watched large Russian babushkas move to and fro, bringing plates of caviar and vodka. Conversation was stilted, but after a few glasses of vodka the mood changed. The officers became jolly and chatty and, as the vodka made more rounds, their faces became flushed and leery. We girls eyed each other anxiously. Then some awful music blared from speakers and the officers dragged us to dance. Their drunken, amorous advances, smelly breath, slobbering kisses and incessant bottom pinching were disgusting. Revolted after dancing with a sweaty fat officer, I escaped back to my seat next to a general, who had not moved all evening. He sat rigid and silent, with eyes fixed on his vodka glass. He wore so many medals, his chest looked like an armoured breast plate. Out of politeness, I asked why he didn't dance. At first there was no reaction, but slowly he turned, fixed vacant eyes on me for a moment, then began to speak. His voice was flat and lifeless. 'You ask why I don't dance? Did I ever dance? I can't remember. I was nineteen when I joined the army. My whole life has gone by on the battlefield. I was wounded at Stalingrad and have seven bullets inside my body. I have seen many comrades die. I have a wife and two sons whom I never saw grow. I didn't see their first steps nor hear their first words. In thirty years, I have spent only few months with my family and am a stranger to them. I am in constant pain from the bullets. Nothing can relieve it. So, you ask, why don't I dance? How could I dance?'

*Something has happened to my understanding that
now makes my heart full of wonder and kindness.*

Hafiz

FRIENDS AND FAMILY

At weekends, I used to go with my classmates for long walks in the forest near Mount Vitosha, where we would often end up sitting on the ground, our backs propped against a tree, discussing the meaning of life. I can still picture our group dreaming of the future, as the indifferent leaves fell on our passionate heads. One afternoon after school, Lidia, the most liberated amongst us, made an announcement. 'Let's go to the sea this summer without our parents!' Holiday without supervision – what could be more exhilarating? The idea took hold, and we could think of nothing else. When one of the girls found out that friends of her family knew of a village on the coast, this became our destination. We found how to get there by train and bus, and then it was time to take the next big step. 'No way,' my parents declared in unison, 'you are going nowhere, is that clear?' But my constant pleading and tears finally softened them. My friends overcame similar resistance and finally victorious, we waved our parents goodbye at the station. The poor passengers in our compartment had to bear with five overexcited girls, screeching and giggling for eight hours all the way to the coast.

The first taste of freedom was intoxicating. I remember nothing of the bus journey to the village, nor how we found our accommodation, nor how we managed to feed ourselves. The only memory I have, was feeling very grown up and blissfully happy. The village was a mile away from the sea. Every morning we walked through the fields to an empty beach, a paradise of golden sand – all ours. There was a disused jetty with missing planks which we would jump over to sit at the end, look at the sea and dream, our feet dangling over the water. Long idyllic days followed, full of laughter, swimming and sunbathing. At sunset we would go back to the jetty and read to each other the strange fairy tales of Hans Christian Andersen, then watch an extraordinary spectacle I haven't seen anywhere else – the sea changing from dark blue to mother of pearl, paler and paler as the sky darkened, stretching to the horizon illuminating everything until the night finally swallowed the last glimmer of light.

One evening, passing through a corn field on the way to the beach, we were tempted to pick some. We collected wood, made a fire and sat on the sand around it like natives. We peeled the cobs while waiting for the flames to subside, lulled by the crackling sounds of burning branches and the lapping of the waves. Suddenly one of the girls jumped up in panic. 'Look, look, there is a man on the beach. He is coming towards us. God, what are we going to do?' We all stood up in alarm. We hadn't seen a soul on the beach the whole time we were there. Had someone seen us stealing the corn? There was no time to hide it now. We stood petrified, fixed on the strange apparition approaching. As he came nearer, it became clear he was not a local peasant. He wore a hat, had a rucksack on his back, and was smiling broadly. 'Good evening girls! I see you have lit a fire. Do you mind if I join you? I have been walking the whole day.' Speechless, we nodded and made a space for him by the fire. He unfastened his sack and brought out something wrapped in newspaper. 'I see you have corn, could I make an offering to the feast?' Inside the paper was a fish. 'I caught it today and would be deeply honoured if you accepted it as a humble gift.'

His gentlemanly manner melted our initial fear. Intrigued, we sat in silence and watched our unexpected visitor take an iron grill out of his bag, place it over the ashes and, with great care, arrange the corn and the fish on the top. Good looking and composed, he seemed skilled and at home in nature. As the aroma of the fish and corn filled the air, our admiration grew. We couldn't take our eyes off his handsome face lit by the fire. Our last reserves fell when he produced a pipe and proposed that we smoke a round of peace. 'On my walking expeditions, I always share the pipe of peace before and after my meals as a small gesture of thanks for what we are given.' With elaborate yet elegant gestures he distributed the food, which we ate in silence. Then followed the pipe of peace, as if we were taking part in some sacred ritual. Enraptured, as the pipe passed from hand to hand, we were completely in his thrall.

'Now is the time to introduce ourselves. I must confess that I am very impressed by you. It's not often I meet young girls enjoying nature's beauty in solitude instead of joining the noisy crowds at the sea resort just twelve kilometres from here. You are special and I applaud you. What are you studying?' Hearing we were all musicians, he exclaimed: 'It's clear now, of course, you know how to listen!' As the night fell, he told us that he was a history professor spending his summer walking through different parts of the country, sleeping under the stars and avoiding town whenever possible. 'I started my walk today with a dear friend, planning to follow the coast from the tip of the Black Sea down to the Turkish border. Unfortunately, on our first day my friend fell and broke his leg. A kind man took us by car to the nearest hospital where they put his leg in plaster. So, he had to go home. I continued the journey alone and here I am after ten hours' walk. Meeting you seems a good omen. Were you waiting for me?'

We had never come across anyone like him or heard of someone sleeping under the stars. It was fascinating and romantic. We bombarded him with questions, how it felt walking alone in the forests, was he not frightened by animals? How did he decide where to camp? We listened to his adventures late into the night. It was like a living fairy tale, opening door after door to a world we had no idea existed. 'It is the best way to discover and know a country. I hope you do the same one day.' He stood up, putting the rucksack on his shoulder. 'Now it's time to say goodbye but first we must put the fire out. Remember never to leave without doing so, it's very important.' We smothered the embers with sand, shook hands with him and wished him luck for the journey. Touched to tears by his free spirit and sad to see him go, we stood still until his solitary figure had vanished into the darkness.

Back in Sofia among my friends, couples were forming and dissolving with the speed of lightning. I was suddenly no longer Rumen's confidante; he left his girlfriend and declared I was his true love. This dizzying state lasted for quite some time until we bumped into a wall – my father. Rumen smoked. My father didn't like it, and that was that. 'I forbid you to see him and as long as you live under my roof, you do as you are told.' I became an accomplished liar using a network of friends to cover for me. It was a dangerous game: for four years we met secretly, hiding in the shadows, avoiding my father at all costs. I resented him intensely. My mother was on my side, but he was stubborn, and nothing could change his mind. His obstinacy and ill temper made life at home very difficult. I now wish I had understood him better.

My father was born into a humble family. His own father had died when he was young, leaving his mother to bring him up along with two sisters. I later learned that he had played the clarinet and was a schoolteacher before studying medicine in Austria. He had gone with no money and not a word of German – only a suitcase full of food. He managed to graduate and returned a doctor. Quite an achievement. He had been married before meeting my mother, but never talked about it. He was secretive and taciturn and everything I learned about his life came in small bits. There was an old sofa in our flat with a drawer we were not allowed to open. It was full of precious things he had collected in case they came in handy one day; plugs, old batteries, rusty nails, cords, and amongst all this, the complete works of Dostoevsky, to whom I was introduced aged eleven when quarantined with chicken pox. My father had handed me Crime and Punishment, a most inappropriate choice that plunged me into a world of Russian gloom. What cheered me up was a tiny white mouse with pink nails and red eyes, which peeked out from the drawer when he opened it. Startled from what must have been its private home for some time (and having chewed many pages of Dostoevsky) it had the aura of a very enlightened creature.

My father was a very contrary man: against ownership in fascist times yet when socialism came to power, he bought an apartment. As if this wasn't hard enough to finance, he also acquired land at the foot of Mount Vitosha. My mother was furious, there was no money to buy clothes or shoes for us. In spite of this, he bought yet another piece of land by the Black Sea. 'I want to give our children a chance to live in nature. It is more important than clothes.' He was right. It gave us the chance to spend our weekends breathing mountain air and to be by the sea in the summer. Nothing seemed impossible for my father. The more difficult the task the more determined he became. Two things my parents did have in common – our education and a terror of deep water. My brother and I would swim out into the sea, while they stood helpless on the shore desperately calling us to come back. However, the quarrels increased. We had no coats for the winter – but father kept buying materials for the house by the sea. Then my grandmother (on my mother's side) came to live with us. A cramped and fractious home became almost unbearable. There was hardly a thing she would not criticise, and she gave continuous unwanted advice. 'Look at you,' she would say eyeing me disapprovingly, 'with that big smile of yours, you will never find a husband.' 'How should I smile?' I would ask.

'Make your mouth the shape of an 'O', and keep it firmly held there when laughing. Otherwise, you will get wrinkles.' 'Your hair is so messy no one will like you. You must part it in the middle and braid it around your ears.' Every day she found things to disapprove of – my short skirts, my shoes, even the way I walked.

Grandmother

Poor grandmother, her life must have been tough. She had seven children one of whom had died young. By the time my mother was born, the oldest was twenty years her senior. Without electricity or running water, she cooked, wove carpets, spun wool, made bed covers, blankets and clothes for all the children. And, as if that was not enough, she crocheted and embroidered by candlelight late into the evening, waiting for my grandfather to fall asleep and not give her another child. She must have been pretty as a young girl, blue-eyed and tall, but was forced to marry my grandfather, twenty years her elder. She used to say: 'My marriage was nothing to talk about, just bearing children and looking after them. Never a moment for myself.' 'Then, be happy no one will marry me with my big smile!' I would say and beam at her.

During the years of rationing after the war, we received aid from America. I have a vivid memory of two brown boxes appearing in our flat one day, and how we ripped them open. There were things we had never encountered before – bars of chocolate, tins of dried milk, powdered eggs, cocoa, even a green dress which was just my size. I could hardly bear to take it off. Among the treasures was a big bag of chocolate drops over which my brother and I fought. Grandmother hid it so well that it was never found again. I still have an irrational craving for chocolate drops.

Grandfather

Grandfather had died long before I was born. I discovered only recently from a cousin that he wrote poetry and had wanted to be a sculptor. He was even offered a scholarship to study sculpture in Italy but was prevented by his parents who did not consider it a proper profession. So, he worked as a post office administrator. But he continued writing poetry, encouraged by an actress friend who appreciated his poems and kept them in a box until her death. After she died her daughter found these poems, and offered them to my mother, who to my great regret, refused. I would have loved to read them. Their oldest son, my uncle Simeon, was a self-taught philosopher, vegetarian, yogi and mystic. He was tall and blond with an innocent babyish face, and was obsessed about the end of the world, which annoyed my father no end. I was fascinated by his stories, though his visits would induce nightmares of the earth bursting into flames or dissolving into a black hole.

By contrast, my uncle Asen, *the holy man* as we called him, was short, kind-hearted and cheerful, with a constant smile on his broad moon-like face. His life was full of hardship, but nothing could break his spirit or wipe the smile off his face. A protestant minister, he baptised many Jews during the Nazi regime to save them from deportation. Rumours of these baptisms reached the ears of the Gestapo and he was arrested in the middle of a sermon and stripped of his priesthood. He became a lawyer, then, during socialism, was accused of being an enemy of the communist regime and imprisoned. Being resourceful and speaking six languages, he somehow managed to support his family and was even employed as a translator for sports teams on tour abroad. In his old age, he was allowed to visit New York to see his son Mihail who had become a well-known sculptor. Here he stayed for a year and translated the Bible into modern Bulgarian, copies of which he managed to smuggle back to Bulgaria and distribute secretly. I still have his translation.

My beloved uncle Christo was an artist. Tall and handsome, he worked as a stage designer for the Opera House in Plovdiv. Visiting him was always a special treat. As a child, I never had a dolls house, so would marvel at the miniature sets he produced for the stage – tables, chairs, little velvet sofas, even chandeliers. Later on, I would watch him paint in his studio. I sat behind him for hours drunk on the smell of turpentine and oils. He would take me to the market, fill a basket with fruit, vegetables and flowers, which he then arranged on a table as a still life. I owe my love of painting to him.

My aunt Velka was something of a mystery. She was a good housekeeper and a great cook, but monstrous. A cigarette hanging between her bright red lips, a coffee by her side, she badmouthed, schemed and threatened to sue everybody around. Was she an evil spirit or a witch? No one could tell. Her husband was a railway engineer, quiet and kind, and a stutterer, which I am sure he had become by living with her. Her two sons were very obedient and well behaved, while she was nasty and controlling, and interfered with their relationships. The girls they chose were all prostitutes according to her. She dug into family histories for proof, or forged letters from imaginary lovers, plotting non-stop. She sued my mother, her brothers, the whole family, and the world at large. Always unsatisfied with the outcome of her court cases, she turned to spiritual séances. When her younger son married against her will, she became vile, hiding their wedding presents and making their life hell. The last time I saw my poor cousin was at his deathbed. He was dying of cancer. 'She has called me, you know. She died three months ago, and I have been ill since then. She won't let me live.' Velka was the only evil person I have ever met.

My mother, on the other hand, had the sweetest nature. Beautiful, with unusually deep blue eyes, she had a lovely smile and great charm. She was refined and gifted, spoke perfect English and had a beautiful singing voice. Under different circumstances she could have been a pianist, singer or actress. She was romantic by nature, a lover of books, poetry and music, who married, as did her mother, a man much older than her, stubborn, practical, fond of wine, good company and climbing mountains. She was like the leaves of a tree; he was the trunk. The slightest wind would stir the leaves, while the trunk did not move. Though very rational, for some strange reason, he hated paprika, which my mother loved, as did the rest of us. She had to cook his meal separately. If by chance the serving spoon from our pot touched his, he would erupt like a volcano. My parents argued endlessly but were funny as well. Father's stubbornness was legendary: if an idea came to his head, no one could change his mind. 'I want to demolish the wall between these rooms,' he said one day to my mother's dismay, 'It will be better to have one large room rather than two small ones.' 'Don't you dare even think of doing such a thing! We are four people living in three rooms, why on earth reduce them to two?' We were all against his idea and fought until he gave in. But a few months later, we came back from a trip to find him standing in a pile of debris, smiling sheepishly. The wall had gone, leaving a great gap on the parquet floor between the rooms. Mother screamed and cursed, wild with rage, but he kept smiling, waiting for the storm to blow over, which eventually it did. Once the mess was cleared and the hole in the parquet floor filled, the new arrangement was a big improvement. I think they both enjoyed fighting – it was their paprika of life.

But, eventually they filed for divorce and went to court as sworn enemies, after which they had a drink to celebrate the separation and returned home best of friends. Peace was restored and I breathed a sigh of relief as life continued in a much more relaxed manner. Not long after, my father had another idea, which again annoyed my mother. 'You must go to University,' he insisted. 'Are you crazy? A student at thirty-eight? What makes you think I could ever pass exams at my age?' 'Nonsense! Age has nothing to do with it, how do you know unless you try?' She would change the subject, but he kept on, laughing at her objections until she finally gave in. What followed were the happiest and most productive years for her and for all of us. He was right again. At the same time as I entered the Music Academy, she started University to study English and Philology. Our dining table was piled with books and papers, we all did homework together. She became young and cheerful again and was adored by her fellow students. Our house was filled with fascinating discussions about English literature, novels, drama, poetry, even grammar. After her dissertation on the verb *to do*', she became a professor and later translated many works from English into Bulgarian, including a biography of Oscar Wilde. Thanks to my father's insistence she flowered and had a career of real fulfilment.

When I left home, she was teaching at the University, and my father was spending his time by the Black Sea, planting vegetables, tending his tiny vineyard and making wine from the most delicious, sweet grapes. Sometimes she would send a telegram 'I am bored!' and he would come home. They would play backgammon and argue until she had had enough and send him back. Many years later, they remarried (for property reasons) but not much changed. Even at the age of eighty, he got so angry he did not speak to her for almost a year. 'He just sits at the table eating the food I cook,' she would tell me on the phone. 'Nothing can change this piece of rock I married!' she would say, laughing. When she died my father was heartbroken. I managed to return home (having been stranded on a Scottish island by violet storms) to find him in deep mourning. He had placed flowers and candles in front of her photograph, which he had enlarged to life size. 'What a pity you never gave her flowers when she was alive, it would have pleased her very much!' 'But I always gave her flowers! (He never did.) 'Our marriage was the best you could have!' I could sense my mother smiling from above. He even arranged a memorial service for her in church, an unbelievable gesture for such a non-believer. I will never forget the sight of him during the service, candle in hand, tears in his eyes. He recorded the singing of the choir and played it from then on, every time I visited. She was the love of his life, he told me, and even if the marriage boat often capsized in stormy seas, she was for him the only one.

BACK TO BACH

Entering the competition

In 1964, my last year at the Academy, I was chosen to represent Bulgaria at the Bach International Competition in Leipzig. I practised intensely and spent sleepless nights with his fugues running through my head, getting stuck, then jumping out of bed to check the score. The list of works we had to prepare was demanding – preludes and fugues, suites, fantasies, concertos. It was my first exposure to the world outside Bulgaria. I was anxious and scared, but still excited about the competition and most of all, excited to see the Thomaskirche, where in the last years of his life Bach was cantor, and where he composed the Passions and many cantatas. When I finally found myself by the church with his statue in front, I dissolved in tears of awe and gratitude. They continued to fall as I went inside and stood by his grave.

The weeks of the competition coincided with a festival of Bach's sacred music: performances every evening of his passions, cantatas, oratorios and organ music. Deprived of his church music at home, this chance felt like a real gift from God. The first concert was his great St Matthew Passion, written in 1727, first performed in Thomaskirche a century after his death. I was lucky enough to hear it now in this very church, alongside my mother, who had been allowed to join me. It was her favourite piece, which she had sung (under the baton of our beloved Dimo) when a student at the American college near Sofia, before communism. Even mentioning the name of this college could later get you in trouble. No wonder we were both in such an emotional state. I remember being impressed by how many people had the score open on their knees, ready to follow the performance. As we sat waiting for the opening notes, I felt as if my heart would burst. I don't think anyone in the packed church could imagine what it meant to us attending a performance of the Matthew Passion in Bach's church. Again, I even felt grateful to the communist regime – forbidding the sacred made it even more profound. Holding hands, we listened for three and a half hours, spellbound, unable to hold back the tears which streamed down our faces.

The next day I went to practice at the Leipzig Academy. In the room on the wall opposite the piano there was a portrait of Bach. As I practiced nervously, I looked up and was sure he smiled at me. I felt so uplifted that I went to the first audition walking on air. Passing through a garden on the way, I sat on a bench to collect myself before going on stage. Then something inexplicable happened. Looking up at the sky while humming the fugue I was about to play I saw the clouds form into five lines on which the theme appeared in round white notes against the blue sky. Stunned, I watched the notes stretching to the horizon until they vanished. I have no recollection of reaching the Hall, only a vague memory of entering an empty room with a black Steinway, a white bust of Bach by the window and a red curtain with the jury hidden behind it. I felt as if I was carried through that day in Bach's great hands; did mine ever touch the keyboard? When I walked out of the room, somebody ran after me, lifted me in the air, saying something in German I couldn't understand. The next day, he introduced himself. He was the composer of a work we all had to perform in the competition. He called me his queen. 'When you played,' he said, 'I felt the spirit of Bach was in you.' He invited me to meet his family and took me to a music shop in the basement of the house where Robert and Clara Schumann had lived. Here he bought me Bach's complete piano works as a gift.

I sailed through the competition in a heightened state and won second prize. The first prize winner, Ilse Graubin, was a Latvian (then part of the Soviet Union) whom I remember being terrified if she didn't win for 'her' country, and whom my mother and I helped to buy a piano with her prize money before the Soviet state claimed it. My teacher was in the jury and cheerfully told me that she gave a higher mark to the Russian candidate in order to keep favour with the Soviets in the Jury. 'I hope you don't mind not getting the first prize,' she said. 'but this way I'm in a better position to help my pupils in future competitions.' There was a lot of fuss afterwards – newspaper interviews, TV appearances, and a concert at the Opera House where all the winners – singers, violinists, organists, pianists, had to perform. I remember waiting nervously in the wings of the Opera House for my turn to play Bach's Third French Suite. The stage was so enormous, the piano seemed impossibly far away. I thought I would never get to it. I stepped out into a blinding spotlight and could suddenly see myself from above, like a tiny ant sleepwalking towards my fate. I still don't know how I managed to play. My mother told me afterwards that I had walked so slowly she was worried I might faint before reaching the piano. Again, I do not believe it was me who played that night.

After the performance, everything seemed surreal, as if I was in a film. Standing, shaking hands with countless government representatives, unable to understand a word they said, smiling until my face ached, I was glad when the formal part finally finished and it was time for the ball, my first ever ball. I was given a little book with a pink pen hanging from it, where the dance partners had to write their names. I found it charming and old fashioned as in the Russian novels I had read. My book filled quickly, and I danced madly all night, passing from one pair of hands to another, including the incredibly handsome Cantor of Thomaskirche, who even invited me to play the famous organ of the church, the following day. I could hardly believe my luck. Unable to walk after all the dancing, I was carried back to my hotel by members of the Bach choir singing to their queen. I was truly on air. It was overwhelming. The next morning, I played the organ high up under the steep roof of Thomaskirche. The roaring sounds reverberated throughout the church and over the crowd below standing at Bach's grave – an unforgettable experience. I received many gifts at this time. I was even offered a teaching post at the Music Academy in Leipzig. I often wonder what my life would have been if I had accepted that offer and later, often wished I had.

Another gift was that the love my life happened also to be at the competition. He was a teacher of mine. Falling in love with your teacher, how common! I was seventeen, and it left a deep impression on my life. Mitko. He was married of course. His wife was Georgian, petite, with dark fiery eyes and a character to match. They were at the Bach competition in Leipzig and I had the strange but exhilarating experience of being driven back to Sofia with them. Travelling by car was a luxury that only a few could afford, a luxury doubled for me by being with him. We stopped in East Berlin, where the scars of the war were still visible – ruins, bricks and rubble, even on the famous boulevard Unter den Linden leading to the Brandenburg Gate. East Berlin was poorly lit and depressing while through a crack in the Wall I could see the same boulevard in West Berlin sparkling with light and life. The contrast was shocking. East Berlin felt like a city dark with sorrow whilst I was glowing with happiness. We drove on through Czechoslovakia, Hungary, Yugoslavia. I could have travelled forever. I was in love – everything was new and fascinating and beautiful.

Mitko and his wife lived out of town, which meant I had to take two trams to their house for lessons. First, tram number five, then a little yellow tram I was very fond of because it seemed to puff going uphill in sympathy with my breathless anticipation. They were excellent teachers and I loved them both, of course, which further complicated things and threw my mind into confusion. They were helpful in different ways – she was demanding and precise. He, on the other hand, was horribly inspiring, especially when I looked into his gold-flecked green eyes, so deep I drowned in them. Often, when explaining something, his hand would touch my shoulder and a hundred volts ran through me. No need going on, you know the feeling. The problem was, I sensed he loved me too – an unbearably sweet poison. But enough of this story, there is something else I want to say.

They lived on the first floor of a small house along with his mother. He, his wife and son were in one room, his mother in the other. They shared a kitchen and small sitting room where they gave lessons and had their meals. His wife, Julia, did not allow the mother there, she was confined to her room and the kitchen. People lived crowded into small spaces at the time, and they were no exception. Such co-existence made life very difficult. I witnessed many ugly scenes between the two women – trivial things that poisoned the atmosphere. I liked the mother. She was gentle, quiet and good-mannered, in sharp contrast to Julia who treated her appallingly, with constant abusive and cruel remarks. The situation seemed worse each time I went for a lesson. It eventually reached a stage where they were no longer speaking. So Mitko became a messenger between the two. I would hear Julia shout at him – *go and tell your mother to stay in her room when I am in the kitchen, I can't guarantee I won't use the knife in my hand…* or, *ask her to let you know when she needs the bathroom, I don't want to bump into her at any time.* It was painful and upsetting to watch him going from room to room trying to keep the peace.

After the lessons, he would accompany me to the tram. This was sheer heaven. We would walk slowly, he talked poetry and I would listen, beside myself. He would wait for the tram to wave me goodbye. One day, after witnessing a very ferocious outburst from Julia, I couldn't help myself, and on the way to the tram I blurted out: 'How can you bear this situation? I can't understand why you let Julia abuse your mother. She doesn't seem aware of the harm she inflicts.' He looked at me. I was overwhelmed by the sadness in his eyes. We stood in silence for a while before he uttered a sentence I never forgot. *If somebody doesn't have a hand or an arm, would you constantly remind them of it?* I don't think my mind understood his words, but my heart did. I felt sorry for the three of them, locked in that hellish situation.

One day I bumped into him on my way to the Academy. All he said was 'Julia is going away for three days.' Nothing more. I waited the whole time by the phone. He did not ring, nor did I. When we finally met, I told him: 'I waited by the phone every day.' 'And so did I,' he replied. And I must tell you how grateful I am that you didn't ring. We would have fallen into a hole so deep nothing could have pulled us out'.

Julia was becoming increasingly harsh and cold towards me, until she finally confronted me: 'You are not allowed in this house anymore, is that clear?' I was devastated and shed many tears over the unfairness of it all. I hadn't done anything wrong. I hadn't lured him into bed or had any intention of ruining their marriage. But deep inside, I knew she was right. Love is impossible to hide even if not acted upon, which in some ways must have been even more threatening. I cried for months, tossed between anger and despair, praying for a chance at least to say goodbye before I left to study in Rome. He must have heard my prayers as, a week before my departure, I saw his car stop in front of my house. Our last sad, tender conversation happened there. The final goodbye left me heartbroken. But even at seventeen I knew, and thankfully he did too, that this love was impossible. For years after, while living in Rome and later Geneva, I had the same recurring dream: we would meet by chance in some unknown, sunlit place, and overwhelmed with joy I would run into his arms. It was dangerously vivid. At first, I tried to stay as long as possible in the dream, savouring its sweetness, but through the years, and it took many, I realized it always came as a warning. Something awful happened every time I had the dream – illness, disappointment, injury. I began to fear it, waiting for the inevitable fallout.

I was married with children, when I first returned to Bulgaria. It was good to see my family and friends, but most of all I wanted to see *him*. I asked my cousin to arrange a meeting. They had moved into a much larger house with an impressive garden. We parked our car at the gate. Julia was standing at the door and welcomed us in. The years hadn't changed her, she looked exactly the same. I heard somebody playing, 'Mitko is giving a lesson and will shortly be with us.' She asked me about my studies and seemed genuinely pleased for me and full of praise for my achievements. Then, he entered the room. Our greeting was awkward. We avoided looking at each other. I was so uneasy and tense it was a relief when he proposed we all go to the garden and pick some of their strawberries, which were very fragrant and sweet that year. Then, he put a strawberry in my mouth and our eyes met. Heavens, how was it possible? I was drowning again. After tea, Mitko and Julia accompanied us back to our car. We had only one brief moment together. 'I dreamed of meeting you for sixteen years', I said. 'And I', he whispered, 'know that God exists because of you.' That was all we had time to say before the others joined. Driving away, I watched him recede into the distance. I never saw him or had the dream again.

I came back from Leipzig triumphant, as if I had conquered Mount Everest. There were more interviews and pictures in the papers. People stopped to congratulate me in the streets. But soon, I discovered the cruel pitfalls of success. To continue with my career, it was almost obligatory to become a member of the Communist Party, which I was not prepared to do. Also, rumours had spread that I had won the prize by sleeping with members of the jury, something which hurt me deeply. My chamber music teacher gave me wise advice, seeing me in tears one day. 'Listen my dear, the sooner you learn, the better. Once you are in the spotlight, people will say terrible things about you, but how much you allow them to hurt you depends only on you, so stop it now!' She was right. After I graduated from the Academy, the glorious time on Mount Olympus ended as quickly as it had come. I wanted to study with Heinrich Neuhaus in Moscow, the teacher of my idol Sviatoslav Richter, but unfortunately, he died that same year. There was a great teacher in Buenos Aires, where my aunt lived, but the authorities did not give me permission to go there. Once again it was Bach who opened the door for me. A member of the jury in the Bach competition, had written a letter to the Bulgarian authorities, asking permission to let me study with him at Santa Cecilia in Rome. I still do not know how it happened, as I never met him or even knew who he was. A whole year passed before I got permission to try for a scholarship in Rome (without which I could not have studied there). After the initial joy, the realisation that I had to leave home also hit me. It felt like a kind of death. I was dreamy and romantic, with a close circle of friends and family and totally unprepared for a life in the West. The last months before my departure I spent cuddled in bed with my mother, crying like a baby, terrified to be taking a one-way ticket into an unknown future.

On a wintry day in January 1966, those I knew and loved, parents, cousins, aunts and uncles, teachers and friends, were all standing on the platform with flowers in their hands, smiling reassuringly. I was leaving with fifteen dollars in my pocket, not a word of Italian and no return ticket. Blinded by tears, I could hardly see the faces of those who hugged me, kissing me goodbye. I can still hear the last words my father said in a trembling voice: 'Never come back, do you hear? Never come back. Better to sweep the streets, but live in freedom!'

I stepped up into the train and stood at the window. As I watched everybody crying and waving, I felt I was witnessing my own funeral. Then, a piercing whistle, the slamming of doors, the shriek of wheels; the train shuddered and moved slowly forward in billows of smoke. Leaning out of the window I stood until the faces on the platform dissolved into a mist. I was as frozen and numb as the landscape outside. The train's desolate whistle echoed across the white emptiness under a leaden sky. The wheels repeated rhythmically *…alone, alone… never come back… no return…* I felt nothing. What did I do after that? I do not know. Can the dead remember?

ITALY

From all that was familiar I broke away.
Now I am lost without a place, wandering.
With no music, like a fool I dance and clap my hands.
How am I to live?

Rumi

The train stopped at Venice. I looked out of the window in anticipation, but everything was hidden in a thick, milky fog. There were a few hours before getting the connection to Rome, so I dragged my heavy suitcases out of the station, hoping to catch a glimpse of the famous city, but couldn't see further than a few metres ahead. I went forward and suddenly found my foot poised above water. One step further and I would have fallen into the canal. Shocked, I returned to the station. If I had drowned, would anyone have found me?

The overcrowded waiting room was filled with women and children, all speaking at the same time. I felt helpless. Fearful thoughts kept running through my head – *would I find the right train… what happens if there is no one to meet me in Rome… I want to go back home… it would have been better if I had drowned…* 'Treno per Roma?' I managed to ask one woman. She pointed to a platform and with huge relief I saw ROMA on the train. It was due to arrive at midnight. I spent the next eight hours worrying if I would be met at such a late hour. When I finally stepped off the train, there was nobody. I began to shake. Then I spotted two elegant figures walking towards me. A friend of my mother's had a sister married to an Italian. It was for her that I had to carry the heaviest suitcase, filled with gifts from her family. We exchanged polite greetings. It was a relief to speak Bulgarian after being silent for days, unable to understand a word. They led me to a smart Ferrari, parked in front of the station. 'If you are not too tired, we would like to show you the city.'

Rome by night was like a stage set. We glided through brightly lit boulevards and magnificent piazzas with fountains – Piazza Navona, Piazza di Trevi, Piazza del Popolo – it all seemed like a dream. Where were the dim-lit streets and cracked pavements of Sofia? The shock continued when we got to their flat. Full of exquisite antique furniture, Persian carpets, beautiful paintings and exotic plants, I never imagined people living in such luxury. On the table, there was a tray of canapés and a bottle of champagne. 'Come, help yourself and tell us the news from Bulgaria.' They listened to my stories nodding and commiserating: 'How sad, it seems communism has brought much misery!' My head was spinning from the champagne, the long journey and the tour of Rome and I must have looked tired, so the wife showed me to my room. I was speechless – it had an antique bed, starched linen sheets, fluffy white towels folded on it and a pink marble bathroom. I felt like a princess in a fairy-tale until I saw my smoke-smudged and tear stained face in the mirror. No wonder my hostess offered to run me a bath, maybe she was worried I might dirty her perfect house. Stretching on the soft bed after a lavender-scented soak, I fell into a deep sleep for the first time since leaving home. The next morning, I was taken to the breakfast room. Sunlight sparkled on a silver coffee pot set around with pastries, crusty buns and jam. What a magical way to begin life in Rome! After breakfast, the wife offered to drive me to my lodgings. The address had been given to my parents by a friend who knew somebody in Italy, who once had a friend who knew a pianist living there… I had no idea where we were going. We got lost a few times down crowded narrow streets, far from the smart area where she lived. When we finally found the street, she stopped in front of a shabby looking building. My heart sank. We went inside and climbed the staircase. I remember standing in front of a black door, a dog barking hysterically behind. After some time, a face appeared behind the door chain.

A young woman with curly black hair and dark eyes, looked surprised at first, but let us in holding onto her dressing gown. 'Sono Anna Maria'. She had a high-pitched voice just like her dog. I stood, glued to the spot, paralysed by the incomprehensible words, the barking and by a strange, dishevelled woman who was standing behind her. *This can't be real… this is not happening to me…I'd rather die than live in this mad house…* Then I saw my hostess leaving. I panicked. I wanted to fall on my knees and beg her not to go but before I could open my mouth she was gone, and the door shut behind her. I struggled to hold myself upright. A scream mounted and lodged itself in my throat, tears pressed against my eyelids. As if looking down from above, I saw myself following Anna Maria to my room, which was so horrible that I nearly fainted. Was it only an hour ago that I was having breakfast in luxury or was it a dream?

Our flat in Sofia was small but at least had central heating and plenty of hot water. This old house was clearly built to keep the sun out. It was dark with cold tiled floors, no carpets and no heating. Everything in the flat was black or white – tables, chairs, the upright piano. The only colour in the room came from one red bar of a small electric heater. The kitchen was basic – one ring gas cooker where you boiled a pot of water to wash. Black and white tiles led to my tomb-like room. There was only space for a small bed and a tiny black cupboard. A grimy window looked onto an inner stairwell. There was a damp, musty odour in the room, which made me feel sick. I wanted to die. I sat on the bed with my suitcase beside me, in shock. I don't know how I managed that first night – wrapped in my overcoat, shivering in the cold bed.

Alipi

The next morning, I somehow found my way to Santa Cecilia. Once there, it seemed deserted. I came to an empty hall with no idea where to go next, whom to ask about my exam, or in what language. Then, a man walked in, looked at me for a moment and said in Bulgarian: 'You're Melita Kolin, aren't you? What are you doing here?' He was very tall, with a narrow face and deep-set green eyes. He introduced himself as Alipi Naidenof. I knew of him as a conductor but had never met him. I must have looked as if he'd fallen from the sky. 'You seem lost, can I do anything for you?' he asked kindly. I could hardly believe my luck – a Bulgarian angel appearing just at the right moment. He took me to the office and helped me fill all the forms for the entrance exam, which was happening in two weeks. Overjoyed by this unexpected meeting we left the Academy together, and wandered the streets, talking nonstop. He asked where I was staying and offered to take me there. I told him I had a room on Via Santa Maria Maggiore. He looked flabbergasted. 'That's unbelievable! I live on the same street.' When we got there, it turned out his house was just over the road from mine. How was it possible that in the whole of Rome we were next to one another? He pointed to his window opposite my front door: 'That is where I live. Incredible!' He invited me in, to my great relief, as going back to my room terrified me. Only when he told me he had hardly eaten in the last month did I run back to get some cheese and salami I had brought from home.

We spent the afternoon talking nonstop. 'You can't imagine how humiliating it is for me to live on a miserable scholarship at my age.' he complained. 'I never wanted to come here in the first place.' 'Why did you?' 'It's a sad story. I was artistic director of the Army Ensemble, which I not only established but put on the map. My mistake was to get rid of incompetent players. I realized too late that sacking members of the Communist Party was overstepping the mark and I am paying the price. I was sent to Rome as a punishment!' 'Why is this punishment when so many musicians would give anything to study in Rome?' 'I've been forced to leave my family and career and am in exile. I am thirty-five and it is hard at my age to live like a starving student. On top of this, I find the Italians shallow, lacking in depth and discipline.' He painted such a gloomy picture that I felt increasingly depressed. 'If this is so, I don't want to study here either.' 'Oh, wait. There are good things too, you will see. Tomorrow, I'll take you to the class of Maestro Ferrara, who is a genius. We can even go to hear the Santa Cecilia Orchestra tonight if you are not too tired, but the walk to the hall is more than an hour.' Anything to avoid returning to my room. By the time we arrived at the hall, my legs were wobbling. I was also dizzy, desperately needing some food. I had never seen so many smartly dressed people and felt out of place in my shabby coat. A wave of expensive perfumes wafted through a fashion show of mink coats as high-heeled ladies hurried past me, gesturing and talking loudly. The noise didn't subside much even during the concert. There was a jangling of ladies' bracelets, clicking of bags opening and closing, sweets being unwrapped and offered around. It made me feel as though we were in a circus. The concert was disappointing too, the orchestra sounded unrehearsed and out of tune. Alipi's complaints began to make sense. On our way back we passed the Coliseum. At that time, anyone could just walk in. Alipi took me through the arches into the immense arena, and described with great gusto what had happened there, pointing at the vaults where lions were kept and unleashed upon the Christians in front of cheering crowds. His descriptions were so vivid that I could almost hear the lion's roar and the shouts of the crowd, even the silence of the dead. In the darkness the place filled with ghosts. I couldn't bear it, ran out and have never since been inside. It was past midnight when we reached our street; my first day in Rome was the longest of my life.

I got into bed fully dressed yet unable to fall asleep; the impressions of the day were whirling through my head. When finally I began to drift off, a strange figure appeared in the dark, and a dishevelled head leant over me and pulled something from under my bed. I was in a cold sweat unable to make a sound. I stared in terror at the apparition until it vanished behind the door dragging something behind it. Opening the door in the morning, I tripped over a body wrapped in rags. In the kitchen, Anna Maria saw my terrified face and explained something to me that I couldn't understand. The same thing happened each night. I couldn't sleep until the strange apparition had come and gone. I told Alipi about it, so he asked Anna Maria, and all became clear. She had seen a madwoman wandering the streets and given her shelter out of pity. But being short of cash, she had to rent her room. As a result, the poor woman had to keep her rugs under my bed and sleep outside my door. Anna Maria then told the woman's tragic story. She had been a proper Signora, married with two children. One day, her husband took the children to see their grandmother. They never came back. She waited the whole day until a policeman came with the shattering news that they had all been killed in a car crash. The shock was so great, she lost her mind and had been living on the streets until Anna Maria took her in. She felt sorry to deprive the poor woman of her room but could not survive on the little money she earned giving piano lessons to children. I could not help but compare Anna Maria, a poor pianist from Bari who had taken this woman under her roof with the charming couple with whom I spent my first night in Rome. They never once called to see how I was in the five years I lived there.

My memories of those first months in Rome are scattered and blurred. What comes to mind are images – Via del Corso… red tomatoes… eating a dry panino in the kitchen… watching Anna Maria squeeze a lemon in her coffee… waiting for letters from home, feeling lost, without identity and cut from my roots. Waking up in that dreary room every morning, stepping over the madwoman to get to the kitchen was something that never failed to disturb. It was also a struggle to practice on Anna's upright piano, but I had to pass the scholarship exam. There was no return ticket. Lucky, I got the scholarship but to my disappointment, it just about covered tuition fees and rent, with nothing left for my keep. During the next six months I experienced real hunger. A strange paradox: I was never deprived of food in Sofia where it was scarce, but in the Rome of plenty, I was starving. Sharing an orange or a piece of bread with Alipi made the hunger bearable. Every morning, before setting out for Santa Cecilia, Alipi and I would decide whether to take the bus or walk for over an hour and have an espresso. The price of both was fifty liras. Of course, we went for the coffee, which meant passing through a tunnel meant only for cars, where the exhaust fumes were so dense that we had to lean against a wall at the other end to recover before going on. But one sip of espresso in our favourite café on the Via Del Corso, and the tunnel was forgotten.

When Alipi presented me to Franco Ferrara I couldn't take my eyes off him; he was incredibly handsome with thick silver hair and noble features. Both charismatic and highly-strung, he would twitch in his chair, hold his head in his hands, hardly able to endure the sounds coming from the orchestra. 'Stop, stop!' he would scream: 'Can't you feel anything? This phrase is a cry of despair. You make it sound like you're ordering a drink at the bar. Again!' After a few attempts with little improvement, Ferrara would jump onto the podium, grab the baton and then... a miracle happened. The music, coming from the same players, reduced everyone to tears. The change was unbelievable. His students then gathered below the podium just in time to catch him falling unconscious into their arms. It was a distressing sight to witness. Ferrara had had a brilliant career but had to abandon it because his nervous system could not sustain the intensity – after three or four minutes conducting, he would faint. Fellini, the film director, came to his aid by asking him to direct music for his films. Master classes with Carlo Zecchi were to begin in a month. Until then I attended Ferrara's class and met Alipi's best friend Mimo, who one Sunday, invited us for lunch at his house.

We arrived at noon to find the table already set for a seven-course meal, which his mother and sisters had prepared all morning. It started with an antipasto, followed by pasta, then chicken, roast meat, vegetables, dessert

Lunch at Mimo's

and fruit. Mimo's Mama piled plate after plate in front of us. By the time the lunch finished, and the coffee served, it was already evening. Feeing rather sick from the culinary overload, we left Mimo's house carrying food in plastic bags to sustain us through the rest of the week. Our Italian Mama seemed determined to put some meat on our bones. This soon turned into a regular Sunday ritual. In Mimo's household it replaced the Sunday mass. The family adopted us, and I have never forgotten their kindness and generosity. We settled into a routine; hungry during the week, coffee after the tunnel, overfed on Sundays.

One morning, to my great surprise, a registered letter arrived from my aunt in Argentina with a cheque folded between the pages. I ran across the road to Alipi waving the cheque, delighted at the prospect of lunch in a restaurant. We immediately headed to the nearest bank. The bank clerk examined the cheque, glanced suspiciously at my Bulgarian passport and declared that the cheque needed at least four weeks to clear. So much for lunch! Suddenly Alipi turned to me, excited. 'Why didn't I think of Papo! He'll help. Let's go!' Long-legged, he walked so fast I could hardly keep up and was still lagging behind when he gestured impatiently at the entrance to a building on Via del Corso. We climbed the stairs to the first floor. Coming from the blinding sunlight outside we entered a room in deep shadow. A plump, bald man in a grey suit wearing gold spectacles was sitting behind a desk. When he lifted his head and smiled at me, the whole room lit up. Alipi told him about the cheque, and barely glancing at it, he said, 'No problem,' and cashed it on the spot. We thanked him profusely and rushed to our café, the money burning in my pocket. Alipi told me that Papo was a Bulgarian Jew, a retired businessman, whose office had become like a citizen's advice bureau. People came to him for help, and being exceptionally generous, he never refused them. Papo's office happened to be above *Alemagna,* the best cafeteria in Rome. Whenever we visited him, he took us there for a treat. I had never seen anything like it before; such elegant décor, platters of exotic fruit, pastries and appetisers in every form and shape, huge rounds of parmesan and haunches of prosciutto, all arranged on the brass counter. Papo would order a variety of things and watch us eat with a big smile. A good listener, he was always ready with advice and encouragement, and soon became like a father to me.

A widower, he shared a house with his wife's unmarried sisters, whom he used to take to exclusive restaurants, often by the sea. He sometimes invited me to join them. The sisters seemed like relics from the last century, tight-lipped spinsters always dressed in black, with old-fashioned hats covered in withered flowers and faded ribbons. They smelled of mothballs. Terrified of the sun, they would wait in the car while Papo brought a large umbrella from the boot to protect their pale complexions on the short walk to the restaurant. I had to restrain myself from laughing seeing this bizarre trio advancing in the sunlight – Papo, plump and short, squeezed between the tall thin spinsters, stretching his utmost to hold the umbrella above their heads. Once seated at table, they said little but ate heartily, never removing their hats. Our weird foursome attracted attention, people from neighbouring tables glanced surreptitiously in our direction. While we enjoyed the delicious meal, Papo would be chasing a lonely olive around his plate, savouring our delight. He gave me the chance to taste the best Italian food. The care he showed for his spinster sisters was touching and I will never forget his kindness to me.

Carlo Zecchi was a celebrated pianist, conductor and teacher, who had studied with Busoni and Schnabel. When the time came to go to his class, I followed six other novices through the corridors of Santa Cecilia, until we all stopped at the same door. Eyeing each other nervously, we entered the room and waited in silence for his arrival. Soon, an elegant man walked in, with a silver-moustache, an old leather bag, a Borsellino hat, fine-cut coat and scarf. He said a cheerful 'Buon Giorno', and then to our bewilderment,

Carlo Zecchi

performed a striptease with unhurried and precise gestures. First went the hat, then the coat and scarf, which he placed carefully on a hanger. Then he took off his jacket, tie and shirt, which he arranged on a different hanger. Now, down to his vest, he reversed the process, pulling out an old shirt from the leather bag, then a large bath towel which he wrapped around his neck. He placed a pencil case on the piano and rolling up his sleeves as if about to begin a boxing match, he turned towards us: 'Now, who would like to be the first to play?' Nobody volunteered, but somehow the striptease had put us all at ease. He asked for our names and right away changed mine to Kolina, which he pronounced so sweetly that I was won over. My turn came to play a prelude by Bach. My hands were shaking. When I finished, he winked at me mischievously, like a child. 'Kolina, isn't Bach a real joy, a never-ending powerhouse of energy? Feel his joy and smile as you play.' His enthusiasm was infectious. Under his spell everything became easy. He was stern at times, but never intimidating and often made us laugh by playing the fool. He had such an enormous palette of nuances at his disposal that it seemed he painted pictures with sound. I was so inspired listening to him playing Schumann that I asked permission to record him. His face darkened: 'No, no, and no! Don't ever dare think of such a thing Kolina, I forbid you!' But each time I heard him play, my temptation increased, and I decided to try in secret. I hid a tape recorder in my handbag, propped it on the chair behind my back and, with a finger on the 'record' button, waited for the right moment. As soon as he started playing, I pressed. Suddenly, the room filled with Charles Aznavour singing *'Ne me quitte pas!'* Infuriated, he shouted: 'Dio Santo, is there no escape from this dreadful music? I can't bear it, call me when it stops.' And he left the room. Our lessons were often interrupted by loud music blasting from passing cars on the narrow street below. I joined the others looking out of the window, then followed the sound around the room, until we all stopped by my chair… I had pressed the wrong button! I wanted the earth to swallow me up. Thank God Zecchi never discovered I was the culprit. I would have been expelled from the class and would have lost him forever.

One day he came into class and walked straight up to me: 'Come on. Kolina, a taxi is waiting downstairs.' I followed him, astonished. The class was left waiting without an explanation. 'We are going to your Embassy,' he said in the taxi and was silent until we arrived. I watched events unfold in amazement. First, we were taken into the reception room where the ambassador gave us a ceremonious welcome with coffee and biscuits. Then Zecchi interrupted the small talk: 'Look here, I haven't got much time, I left my class waiting and I am here in person to make sure this talented girl, who is an honour to your country, can concentrate on her work with me without worrying about her passport. Could you please solve this problem?' The ambassador, taken aback, promised at once to extend my passport. I had no idea how Zecchi knew about my residency issues. In the taxi back, he looked triumphant. 'Right Kolina, now you can concentrate on the piano.' I tried to thank him, but he waved his hand: 'No need. I know these bastards well, so now, back to the class.' A month had gone by and slowly I was getting accustomed to life in Rome, practicing and learning Italian. But I still had not received any letter from home. Longing for news I would often sit on the steps of Santa Maria Maggiore or go inside the cathedral, but never found the solace and peace I used to feel in the Orthodox churches of Sofia. The gilded ceilings and marble columns were impressive but felt impersonal, more like being in a museum. It was vast and cold. I couldn't imagine God being at home here. Nor did I feel at home, I missed my family and old friends terribly, even though I was gradually making new ones.

Alipi lodged with Lucia and her brother Enzo, a small, skinny Napolitano, who worked night shifts at the train station, chauffeuring people to their hotels. Incredibly energetic, he would get home in the small hours after work, and start cleaning the rooms of Lucia's pensione, while she lazed in bed till noon. She spent the rest of the day with her feet up on the sofa, polishing her nails, singing popular songs and watching soaps on TV. Plump, with thick glasses, she was allergic to any kind of work. We often wondered about this strange arrangement. Why was Enzo doing all the housework? One day Alipi confided to me that every night Enzo would open his door when back from work, switch on the light on and offer him a cigarette. 'I find this so irritating I want to slap him. I hate being woken like this. Is he mad?' 'Maybe he is checking Lucia is not in your bed.' I joked, 'Ask him to stop and be firm.' He did, and for some time Enzo left him in peace. A month later Alipi appeared at my door looking very pale. 'You can't imagine what I just saw, it's disgusting.' He was trembling. I gave him a glass of water. 'What happened?' 'I found these bastards making love in the linen cupboard, can you imagine, a brother and sister, how could they do such a thing! I can't even look at them. You must come with me. I can't face them alone.' We heard Lucia singing like a nightingale in the back room. Enzo was nowhere to be seen. But from then on, they held hands openly in front of us. A few months later, Enzo shocked us again: 'I would like to invite you home for tea and present you to my wife and kids.' His house… his wife… children? We were speechless. One afternoon Enzo appeared, beaming, in a smart suit. He drove us to the other side of Rome and parked the car in front of a modern apartment. We went inside and Enzo, fiddling with an enormous bunch of keys in the lift, pressed the button for the fifth floor. When he opened the door of the apartment, we gasped. A young, very pretty woman stood at the door, smiling shyly, surrounded by seven small children, all looking at us with big black eyes. Enzo kneeled ceremoniously at her feet, kissed her hand, and turning towards us, proudly announced: 'I present you my wife Maria and my beautiful children!' The children hung around his neck like a bunch of grapes, kissing him as he recited their names to us. The flat was well furnished, the table set for tea with cakes and sweets. Enzo, presiding at the head the table looked at his wife with moist and adoring eyes. The children were well brought up, the cake was tasty, and the conversation cheerful – like an advertisement for the perfect Italian family. There were more kisses on saying goodbye at the door. We were dumbfounded and, in the lift, asked him what was going on. 'Oh, there is nothing to explain, it's very simple,' he smiled mischievously. 'My wife is La Madonna and Lucia, l'Amore. I couldn't tell you before, that she's not my sister, could I? But what do you think of my wife? Isn't she wonderful? I adore my family and would do anything for them. I am a lucky man.'

As the summer approached, my anxiety increased. Soon my scholarship would run out. What was I to do? Alipi was going back to his family in Sofia and everybody else was leaving Rome. Going home was not an option for me for fear of never getting out again. I was going to be alone in a hot, empty city. And then, a letter arrived. When I saw the name on the back of the envelope, a childhood memory came back. My mother used to talk disapprovingly of my aunt seducing a certain Nasko in Argentina, a man ten years younger than her. She even lived with him and her husband under the same roof. Now, this mysterious lover was writing to me: '*I have heard so much about you from your aunt that I feel I know you. I am coming to Europe soon and it would give me immense pleasure to meet you in person. If you find this agreeable, I suggest we meet in Paris, where thirty years ago, I spent three unforgettable months on my way to Argentina and have wanted to revisit ever since. I would be very privileged to show you Paris and very much hope that you will accept my invitation and, of course, I shall take care of all the expenses…*' I read the letter again and again. Paris? Could this really be true? Since my teenage fascination with French novels, I had always dreamed of seeing Paris. But I needed a passport for France. I ran like mad from one embassy office to another, filling forms, providing photos, reduced to tears by setbacks and dismissals. But somehow, miraculously, the day came that I found myself on the way to Paris. On arrival at Gare Saint-Lazare, a man ran towards me with open arms. 'You look exactly the same as the photo in your aunt's house. It's wonderful to meet you at last. We will have a marvellous time in Paris together.'

What a magical city! White clouds were dancing across the Parisian sky. I took a big breath and felt my lungs expand. No city has attracted so many illustrious poets, writers and artists as Paris, and I couldn't have wished for a more passionate guide than Nasko. Pockets stuffed with books from Molière to Beckett, Nasko, like a detective, steered me on their tracks, through a labyrinth of streets and alleyways from the Right Bank to the Left and onto the Ile de la Cité. We followed Flaubert, Maupassant and Zola through the Latin Quarter, Montparnasse, Place Vendôme, Park Monceau, Folies-Bergère… everything was heightened as though I was walking along the very pages of their books. After dinner in our little bistro, Nasko would read me extracts from novels or stories, to inspire the next day's exploration. Everywhere we went I felt a sense of recognition, a *déjà vu*. My memory of Victor Hugo's Hunchback of Notre Dame was so vivid that climbing the winding stairs to the top of the great cathedral, I could see Esmeralda dancing in the square below through Quasimodo's eyes. Nasko told me the story of each artist as we admired their paintings in the Louvre. Walking in the streets, he would point out landmarks of writers who had lived or died there and read poems or extracts from the novels they had written. One afternoon, he took me to a small, secluded square where once Rodin had a studio. I could almost feel his presence. Over the years I have looked for that place but never again found it.

Our literary explorations ended fittingly at Père-Lachaise Cemetery, the final resting place for so many of our heroes. Here we spent a dreamy afternoon, meandering among the graves of Chopin, Balzac, Rossini, Molière, Proust. We followed the cypress-lined alleys and more names appeared – Colette, Sarah Bernhardt, Isadora Duncan, Maria Callas, Edith Piaf… their spirits filled the air, as we sat in silence under the shade of a tree. I think of Père-Lachaise with gratitude – I had never known a place such profound peace. Waking up each morning in the hotel with croissants and coffee in bed, without a care in the world, was the most precious gift and I can never thank Nasko enough. How clever of my aunt to have seduced him. I too was charmed by his knowledge and enthusiasm and was very sad to wave him goodbye. On the train back to Rome, the thought of Paris glowed like a jewel in my heart.

The next term Alipi and I were housed in a student residence away from the centre. Meals were included, so our time of starvation was over but at a price – the residence was for pupils aged between fourteen to sixteen, and there was a strict curfew. We were locked in the building with the youngsters at nine o'clock every evening. The youngsters often escaped by making ladders out of their sheets while we entertained ourselves with stories. Alipi had these in abundance. He would also describe films he had seen so vividly that if I saw them later, they paled in comparison.

MONTSERRAT

I was preparing for the Maria Canals Competition in Barcelona, working all day in a tiny underground practice room at the student residence. It was soundproofed, with no windows. The ghostly fluorescent light and lack of fresh air left me exhausted. I lived on oranges and biscuits that a kind girl used to bring to my cell. I was so looking forward to Barcelona, and just needed a Spanish visa but it never arrived. The competition had already started. Terribly disappointed, I gave up and stopped practising. Two days later, I received a telegram from Barcelona: *Visa granted. Come immediately. Pensione Goya, Via Laietana, Barcelona.* At first, I thought it was a joke. Missing the preliminary round meant that I was out of the competition, so I ignored the telegram. Then I received a second, urgent one. I packed in a hurry and arrived at the Pensione after a long night and half a day's travel. I felt like a zombie and fell asleep immediately. Other competitors staying at the Goya woke me, combed my hair and bundled me in a taxi to the official reception. We entered a large room, packed with people. I stood confused, in my red coat, when suddenly another red coat approached and greeted me in Italian. 'You must be Melita. So glad you've finally arrived. I have been waiting for you. I am Montserrat.' She was beautiful. Her dark eyes were shining with warmth and affection. She took my hand and it felt delicate and small, like a child's hand. I was immediately drawn to her. 'You are welcome to practice at my house, come tomorrow – here is the address.'

In the morning, I got terribly lost. I took a bus going in the wrong direction, had to find a return stop and wait for the next one back. I arrived an hour later at an imposing iron door, rang the bell and a porter led me through a luxurious entrance hall, with tapestries and flowers, to a lift. He pressed the button for flat five. Montserrat welcomed me at the door of her apartment and took me to a simple sitting room with a mahogany Bechstein grand in the corner. 'I hope you will be comfortable here,' she said, 'if you need coffee or anything else to drink, just ring the bell and the maid will bring it to you.' She pointed to a bell on the wall and wishing me a good practice, left the room. Just as I began to concentrate, Montserrat opened the door with an apologetic smile: 'I am so sorry to disturb you, but I forgot completely that in your absence, another pianist has been practicing here and he's now arrived. Do you mind if I take you up to my mother's flat? She also has an excellent piano.' We took the lift to her mother's apartment where a grand piano faced double doors opening onto a roof garden with fully grown trees and flowering bushes. 'I am sorry for all this trouble, please forgive me,' she kept excusing herself. I reassured her that I didn't mind where I practised. 'You are so understanding, thank you!' But before an hour had passed, she appeared again; a gardener was supposed to water the plants on the terrace, so, would I mind terribly moving to her brother's flat on the third floor because … This time we burst out laughing: 'I am sorry, as you can see, I have run out of excuses. You must think I am mad.' She looked adorable when she laughed. That day I made a tour of four apartments, each one more lavishly furnished than the last, with numerous maids coming and going. I met the whole family, from the oldest brother on the first floor to the father, crowning the top of the seven-story building with, as head of the family, a piano to match.

Montserrat had fought for me to enter the competition. I had to play both rounds in a special audition at midnight. Waiting all day to give a recital in the middle of the night was like waiting for an execution. My new roommates held my hand until I walked on stage and were there when I walked off in a daze, not sure if I played or dreamed I had. They took me in their arms and showered me with praises. That night, we roamed the streets of Barcelona till dawn, dancing and talking in a mix of different languages. I not only won a special prize in the competition, but Montserrat invited me to stay with her and her husband Ramon for another week. I was very tempted but would lose my return train ticket. 'Don't worry, she said, 'we will send you back by plane.' I wasn't sure if I should accept, but my friends encouraged me, so I moved from the Pensione to her apartment. Montserrat's flat was simple in comparison to the lavish ones of her family. It had the same wonderful parquet floors and carved wooden doors, but the walls were empty. There were two sofas with white covers and a wooden table between them, a crooked lampshade by the fireplace, a piano and little else. Bare bulbs hung from the ceilings. When she saw me looking at them, she smiled apologetically: 'We moved here ages ago, just after we were married but we couldn't agree on the lighting, so the subject was dropped!' The Bechstein was the most luxurious thing in the apartment. I also noticed some paintings stacked behind the sofa: 'Oh, that is Ramon. We have a good collection of Spanish painters, but he prefers bare walls. He likes to look at them one by one rather than hanging them on the walls where they become mere background. I must tell you I have no idea why I felt so upset when you didn't come,' she smiled at me, 'this has never happened to me before. Hundreds of pianists have practised in my house since the competition began fourteen years ago, and I've never worried who came or not. But this time, I made enquiries and when I found out that you were denied a visa because of your Bulgarian passport, I was determined to get you here. I fought. It was inexcusable to punish a young pianist and a prize-winner in the Bach Competition, just because of their passport. I did not give up until they agreed to bend the rules and give you a chance. At the same time, I wondered why I was fighting for somebody I had never met. Now I am delighted I did.'

During my stay I had a taste of Spanish life – lunch at two-thirty, supper at ten-thirty, midnight strolls on the Paseo de la Gracia and Las Rambles. I was astonished to see the streets, cafes, and restaurants crowded with people eating and drinking, at one in the morning. I loved their way of life and wished I could stay forever. As the time for my departure approached, my heart sank, and Montserrat's eyes were downcast. There were prolonged silences during our meals. My excitement at flying for the first time diminished rapidly on the way to the airport: I didn't want to leave them. Ramon and Montserrat escorted me right to the steps of the plane. I cried like a baby looking at the two tiny figures on the tarmac until we took off and they vanished. Montserrat phoned me as soon as I got home, and within a month, they had come to visit me in Rome. We couldn't be apart for long. She always knew when I needed to be rescued and would send me a ticket for Barcelona. 'I think it is time for you to come home.' It was the beginning of an extraordinary friendship that lasted until she died over thirty years later.

There are some encounters that change the course of your life. Montserrat was one such encounter for me. I can't imagine what my life would have been without her. She became my best friend, my spiritual mother, and played a great role in my development. Her death was an enormous loss and I still miss her. No one who came in contact with her could ever forget her.

When Montserrat was seventeen, traces of tuberculosis were discovered in her lungs and she was sent to a sanatorium in Davos for treatment. But instead of a cure, the doctors managed to infect her healthy lung as well. Ramon, then her fiancé, had also lost one kidney to tuberculosis. She used to tell me that her father was against her marrying him: 'Marriage between

Montserrat

the two of you, one with one kidney and the other one lung is not a good idea. You'd be better off marrying a strong man.' One beautiful morning in Davos, Montserrat was told she had only a week to live. She turned to Ramon, 'How wonderful the mountains look! Isn't it sad to die in spring when everything seems so glorious?' At which he replied, 'Well, we all have to die, what difference does it makes if at seventeen or seventy?' She was not comforted by his remark but was impressed by his wisdom and strength. She showed me a picture of herself in a newspaper article, *The Swallow and the Dying Girl,* that reduced me to tears. In it, Montserrat was looking up at a nest a swallow had made in the corner of the ceiling of her room. She was stunningly beautiful with shining feverish eyes. Many patients had perished in the Sanatorium during her stay. 'If I were not from a wealthy family, there would have been no problem. Just by spending some time in the Pyrenees as our doctor suggested, I might have been cured. But the Swiss Sanatoriums at the time were the place to be – elegant hotels where doctors experimented on wealthy clientele. Rules were rigid: we had to dress for dinner and pretend everything was normal. The tables were set with silverware and roses in crystal vases. But at night I could hear the sledges carrying the corpses down the mountain. The empty spaces at the tables were quickly filled with new arrivals. Death was never mentioned.' This was the place where Thomas Mann had stayed, which inspired his novel *The Magic Mountain.* If the family doctor had not interfered and persuaded her father to take her urgently for an operation in France, she would have died. She was smuggled secretly in the night across the border and was operated on immediately. It left her with a large hollow in her chest, which she stuffed with padding under her clothes. She never complained, something which I admired greatly. 'Facing death was very fortunate. It made me who I am now.' She was told that having children would endanger her life. She was not to fly and should avoid high altitudes, all of which she totally disregarded. She spent every summer in Mas Aranso, the highest valley in the Pyrenees, survived many flights as well as a miscarriage.

I have never come across a more perfect partnership than that of Ramon and Montserrat. It never ceased to astonish me how two people, so different in character, could be so tolerant and loving. Ramon was a book publisher, a private person, punctual, attentive, a man of few words, who possessed a great sense of humour and impeccable timing. He was usually silent at meals, but when he did speak, the table exploded with laughter; he had a brilliant timing and a great sense of humour. He used to take long walks in the Pyrenees, always with a hat and umbrella or would tuck himself away in a secluded place to read a book. He was not fond of big family gatherings, or of playing games till the early hours, as happened regularly at Mas Aranso, their family home in the Pyrenees. He had an incredible ability to disappear unnoticed. I would be talking to him at lunch only to find his chair suddenly empty.

'How do you do it, Ramon?' I asked him once. 'Well, this is the only way I can survive such a large and noisy family.' Montserrat, on the other hand, was the life and soul of every party; good at all games, witty and entertaining, and fluent in at least four languages. She was the only person that could tell a joke in any of these and still make it funny. Notoriously unpunctual, she seemed genuinely surprised when people complained. One famous occasion, when they were going to the opera, Ramon, after waiting in the lift for a quarter of an hour had gone back to look for her and found her in the bathroom with the maid drying her hair, which she had just decided to wash. With her, it wasn't only a question of ten minutes or an hour, sometimes it could extend to days or weeks.

Ramon used to recount the many occasions when she invited friends for lunch and then forgot. The maid would inform him that visitors were waiting in the salon. He had to receive them, hiding his surprise and inventing excuses for Montserrat. He seemed more amused than annoyed by her behaviour. Once, needing a loan, he had invited the bank manager and his wife for lunch, giving a stern warning to Montserrat: 'Please, make sure to be here this time and be nice to the banker. It is crucial.' She had been very gracious during lunch and all was well until they had moved to the salon for coffee, where, sitting in her usual place on the sofa, she had fallen asleep. To save the situation, he proposed: 'Why don't I lower the blinds, so we can all have a little siesta.' If anybody criticised, he always defended her. 'She wouldn't be Montserrat if she acted differently. I wouldn't like to change anything about her.' She also returned the favour. He drove well on straight roads but was unable to park the car, so he would call when stuck and ask her to take a taxi to come and park for him. Unable to have children herself, she worked with great determination on a project to create villages for orphans and abandoned children. She raised funds and establish these villages all over

Spain. The idea was wonderful – instead of impersonal institutions, she built houses where eight children lived with one 'mother' looking after them, and they joined school and other activities as a normal large family.

The first time Montserrat took me to Mas Aranso it almost never happened. We were together in Barcelona when she announced: 'We will go there tonight, so pack your case.' After supper, she said she had an important meeting in the morning and postponed the journey to the next night. I unpacked. The next night the same thing happened, she was terribly sorry but had to meet someone urgently, and so it went on for a week. Packing. Unpacking. I thought we would never go. Then, after dinner on the last night she said, 'we are leaving after supper' and amazingly, by one in the morning, we were on the road. She was an excellent driver, I always felt safe with her even if she had a tendency to speed. When I asked why she had to drive so fast, she replied: 'I would fall asleep if I drove slowly, which is much more dangerous.' After three hours climbing hairpin bends, we reached the highest point of the Pyrenees and Montserrat, with childlike excitement, pointed to lights below: 'We are nearly there, what you see is Gerona the highest valley in the Pyrenees.' She sped through sleepy villages on our descent and turned off the main road onto a small lane with tall poplar trees. I saw a lit window through the branches and had an overwhelming feeling that I had been there before. It reminded me of a picture in a storybook my father used to read to me as a child, of a little girl lost in the forest at night amongst gigantic trees, seeing a house with a flickering candle in the window. The moment I entered the hall, the pungent smell of polished wood was so familiar that it felt like coming home after a long absence. My room had the same familiar feeling and smell. When I opened the shutters, the stars spilled into the room and the fresh mountain air poured over me like milk and honey. Immense, profound peace enveloped me and, enthralled,

I stayed there, looking at the distant mountains in the pale moonlight for what felt an eternity.

Montserrat's father had bought Mas Aranso, then just a small farmhouse in the Pyrenees, adding another wing at the birth of each of his seven children. By the time I was there, it had been transformed into a large two-storey building, accommodating all the siblings with their families and friends. There were never less than thirty people at the table. The house was brimming with animated conversations. Unable to understand much, I enjoyed listening to the Spanish, which sounded like a cascade of stones rolling down a mountain. The father's absentminded hospitality was legendary. Once when playing golf with a friend, he invited him to lunch, to which the surprised man answered: 'Thank you very much, but I have been staying in your house for a week already.' Mas Aranso was a paradise for me: I had a piano, a pool to swim in and a table in a corner of the garden where I could paint. I loved looking at the high peaks against an intense blue sky in the crisp morning light, something that Montserrat never saw, only rising at noon, when she would have her breakfast. It was an entertainment not to be missed. She started with a grapefruit prescribed by the doctor. She would pile six spoons of sugar on the top to make it edible, put half a spoon of instant decaffeinated coffee into a cup of hot water, add another six spoons of sugar, and dip in it a slice of bread with tomato and olive. 'You are eating too much sugar, Montserrat, it's not good for you,' I would say. She would give me a triumphant look. 'Why not? It's the only thing the doctors forgot to forbid.' Because of her high blood pressure, she was not allowed salt, so separate meals were prepared for her. But after eating them with disgust, she would serve herself the seasoned food as well. 'But Montserrat, you know you can't have that,' her sister would say disapprovingly. 'Of course I know, but it tastes much better.' After a lengthy lunch, some went for a siesta, others for a horse ride or excursion into the mountains. I would paint, waiting for Montserrat to finish her nap, after which we would go for a drive to watch the sunset. By the time she appeared, dressed for the North Pole, the sun was already low. Once in the old jeep, covered in warm jackets and blankets, we climbed high up through stunning landscapes. At these heights, even in August, it is bitterly cold. As the stars populated the sky, streaks of smoke would be rising from the villages below and the air filled with the sweet smell of burning wood and the sound of cowbells. Completely frozen, but exhilarated, we would return invariably late for supper. Around midnight more family and friends would arrive to play games. Then we would move on to the music room, where I played for them into the early hours.

Montserrat was deeply religious; her favourite saint was Teresa of Lisieux, whose little book of writings was by her bed. She was always engaged in some project helping the deprived. She brought home all sorts of stray dogs, some attractive, some hideous and unruly. She would do the same with people; a weird collection would turn up at Mas Aranso, and to the horror of her sister and brother-in-law she would invite them to stay. I suspect she enjoyed the dynamic this unlikely mixture brought to the table. But I once asked her how she could support people who were difficult. I'll never forget her reply. 'It is easy to help people you like. The hard thing is help those you don't. It's my religious practice.' When in Barcelona, she would go every Wednesday with her sister and cousins all dressed in fur coats, to a hill in the nearby countryside for a night vigil. Apparently, the Virgin Mary had appeared to a peasant called Pedro, with messages about the future. Years later, Montserrat took me there. I saw stone steps and a big empty fountain, waiting for a spring that the Virgin had promised would appear. 'Why did they build this fountain when there is clearly no water?' I asked. 'Well, this is the level of Pedro's understanding, he is a simple peasant,' she smiled. 'What can you do? Still, he is a well-meaning man with a good heart.' She called me one night some years later, 'I have a dilemma. You remember Pedro? The Virgin has again appeared to him asking that I go with him to Togo to build a refuge for lepers. I don't even know where Togo is. Somewhere hot in Africa, with no hotels. I don't know what to do. The Virgin has reassured him I'll survive, but my doctor is urging me to have an operation. Apparently, I need a pacemaker. Togo, he says it is out of the question; go if you want to die. What do you think is better – die in Togo or on the operating table?' She seemed worried, but I knew she would go; no sensible argument had ever stopped her. She went to Togo twice and the leper's refuge was built.

Ramon was due a heart operation. His doctor suggested he had a better chance of success in America. Neither he nor Montserrat were keen on going so far, worrying about the flight, which was also dangerous for her. But after long consideration, they took the risk. To everybody's relief, the operation was successful, and she survived the flights. Ramon looked a bit frail when I saw them later, but in good spirits, joking. 'All my life I've hated plastic, and now, there's a plastic tube in my heart. What I want now, is to survive Montserrat for a day only, just to see what she will die from.' As it happened, she survived him for many years. It is strange that unavoidable circumstances prevented me from being at the funeral of my mother, my father and Montserrat, but I was able to attend Ramon's. When the news of his death came, I went straight away to support Montserrat in her great loss. She was devastated. We spend days crying and talking about Ramon. 'I can't forgive myself,' she lamented, 'I did not spend enough time with him. I was too absorbed with my projects or playing cards all night. I wish I had stayed with him instead… now it's too late.' She was inconsolable. A big crowd stood around the monumental family grave. Four men in blue overalls, with cigarettes hanging out of their mouths, were attempting to remove the enormous stone lid on the top, poking it with long iron bars without success. It became clear they were not up to the job.

I whispered to Montserrat: 'Why didn't they open the grave before?' She explained that it could only be done in the presence of the family. The men struggled in vain, swearing, until some members of the family got involved. This took nearly an hour. The sky darkened and it started to rain. 'He loved the rain!' Montserrat whispered to me. The gravediggers lowered a ladder and one of them went down, but reappeared a few minutes later, addressing Montserrat. 'Señora where do you want me to put him, with his mother or the sister?' Startled, Montserrat stuttered; first she said his sister then changed her mind to the mother. The man disappeared again, and soon, we saw with horror, many bones flying out of the grave. Finally, he reappeared, removed the ladder, and the four gravediggers tied the coffin with ropes. An even more bizarre scene then followed. As the coffin was lowered into the tomb, it banged left and right against the walls. Everyone held their breath as it slipped and nearly dropped. I took Montserrat by the hand. She looked calm.

With Montserrat and Ramon

A faint smile appeared on her face as she whispered: 'Ramon is finding all this very amusing – he is watching from above.'

Montserrat loved the night. Her excuse for not going to bed was: 'It's the only time I am left in peace, no phone calls, no people, no demands. All my ideas come at night.' It was true. She would often call me at night, and I miss these precious conversations; no one has ever made me laugh as much as she did. Sometimes she came up with charming requests – singing with a trembling voice something totally out of tune. 'Can you tell me what this is? I know it so well but can't remember. It's going through my head non-stop.' She went on repeating the same unrecognisable tune until I made a desperate guess: 'Is it the third movement of Beethoven's Waldstein sonata?' 'Of course, thank you. Now, I can sleep.' I knew she would still be up for hours. Such a shameless liar! One night, she called. 'You know the Bach concerto, the one for four pianos? I love it but have not heard it for many years. The last time was with Ramon at least forty years ago. I can't understand why it's not played. It is such a beautiful concerto. Do you think you could find three other pianists to perform in Barcelona? I want to hear it once more before I die.' It was a wonderful idea, but very impractical and costly to hire four grand pianos and an orchestra for a piece of music lasting only twenty minutes. No surprise it is rarely performed. But the idea had already taken hold. She hired the Palau de la Musica in Barcelona, found an orchestra and arranged for the pianists (from different countries) to travel and rehearse together. Her idea grew into a great fundraising event for children of the world and was sold out. Organising on such a scale was not easy even for her. But she never gave up and finally heard her beloved concerto again, along with concertos for three, and two pianos. I was immensely happy to take part in what turned out to be her last project. Seeing her shining face at the end of the concert was the best reward I could have. She died a year later.

CONCERTS

In my last year at the academy, Carlo Zecchi handed me the score of a Mozart concerto. 'Here Kolina, you have a month to learn this. You're going to play it with an English orchestra at the Ravenna Festival. I've recommended you to an excellent conductor, a friend of mine, so don't embarrass me. Start practicing at once.' The time was short, and I worked like crazy in the August heat. The concert was to take place in the courtyard of the Basilica San Vitale, famous for its splendid mosaics. I arrived in Ravenna terrified and came to the rehearsal with wobbly legs and stomach tied in a knot. The conductor, Daniele Paris, introduced me to the orchestra: 'Now let's see, who do we have here? This young pianist from Bulgaria, looks pretty anxious to me. But we are not going to eat her, are we?' The players laughed as he led me to the piano. Daniele was sturdy and suntanned with long hair and mischievous eyes full of laughter. After the rehearsal, he invited me with a few members of the orchestra for lunch in a restaurant by the sea. He was so friendly and funny that I finally relaxed. We spent a pleasant afternoon on the beach eating watermelon and swimming. We were all captivated by him.

Concert

After the general rehearsal we again went to the beach for lunch, but as the afternoon wore on, pangs of anxiety hit me. Daniele noticed and came up with a proposal: 'Come, let's perform the whole concerto for the sea. You sing the piano part, and I, the orchestra. The sea is the best listener, give it all your heart.' And, standing with our feet in the water, we sang to the sea. The clouds, like gigantic ears, listened from above. In the evening, when Daniele lifted his baton, he turned to me with a smile and winked. I felt transported back to the beach where we had sung to the waves. It was the best preparation for a concert I ever had and thanks to Daniele's magic touch, Mozart came to life that night. The next morning, we went for a last swim before leaving Ravenna. A violinist from the orchestra told me he was starting a small music festival at his house in Cornwall. 'I hope you will come and play chamber music there one day, so, keep in touch.' He scribbled his address on a napkin – Prussia Cove – the name meant nothing to me.

Back in Rome, I continued meeting with Daniele when his schedule allowed, and had another chance to play a concerto with him and the Santa Cecilia Orchestra. He introduced me to his family and friends, and we spent unforgettable evenings at his house, talking and laughing late into the night, and our connection developed into a treasured friendship so rare in Italy. Once, over a drink after a concert, he told me a fascinating but disturbing story. 'It was in August,' he began, 'I was working on a score and unable to concentrate in the heat. I decided to go for a swim, took the car and drove towards Civitavecchia. But, instead of taking the usual turn off the motorway, I went north, driving on and on, unable to stop until I reached the furthest, I could go, beyond the Arctic Circle. I don't know what possessed me, but I had no choice, and had to go on, as if pulled by a magnet. My disappearance was a shock to everybody. I was declared a missing person, the police were searching for me, they even feared me dead. I came back after three months, confused and unable to explain the reason for my disappearance. Sometimes I feel a cloud comes over me and I lose all sense of reality. Thank God, it's not very often.' Three years later when living in Geneva, I received an invitation from him to play Beethoven's Fourth Piano Concerto with the Santa Cecilia Orchestra. I signed the contract, overjoyed to work with him again and revisit Rome. A week before the concert, I called to make the final arrangements, only to find nobody knew where he was. As endless, frantic phone calls went to and fro, the concert date came and went without a sign of him. He had vanished and I will never know what happened – he is no longer alive.

Every summer there were music courses in different cities and one of these brought me to Venice, the city I had hardly glimpsed on that first lonely journey from Sofia. It was August – Venice was hot, humid and full of tourists. The course was organised by a fearsome man, who ran it with military precision, watching our every step with eagle eyes. We nicknamed him The Fascist. The lessons were held in a large room of Palazzo Vendramin on the *Canale Grande*, where, on the first day, the concierge gathered us in one corner, lifted a tapestry on the wall, and pointing at some faded, brownish stains, whispered: 'See these marks? They are the stains of Wagner's blood that splashed on the wall when he died of a brain haemorrhage.' We bought his story and kept glancing at the tapestry during the lessons, but later discovered that though Wagner did indeed die in that room, it was of a heart attack. We sweated through interminable Monteverdi operas, and spent the nights sitting in the local cafés eating ice cream and drinking cold lemonade, next to foul-smelling canals, waiting for the morning breeze to cool the air. Going to bed was useless – it felt like lying on hot coals. Those nights have remained vivid in my memory; a buffoon entertaining the crowd, dogs, children running around, old men quarrelling over politics, waiters in white aprons balancing trays, old ladies bending tenderly over a baby on the breast of a young mother, a boy with a guitar singing to his friends. After only a few hours' sleep, I was back in the deserted Piazza for breakfast before going to lessons. Sipping my coffee, I witnessed Venice rise from sleep: the sharp staccato of rolling shutters, shopkeepers greeting each other in sleepy tones and sweeping the pavement in front of their shops. I loved the mornings in this golden city of innumerable churches, palaces and mystifying narrow alleys. Come September, the light softened, the tumult died out with the crowds, and Venice seemed to turn inwards as if trying to forget the summer chaos. Autumnal mists crept over the canals, wrapping everything in an atmosphere of eerie nostalgia. It was easy to get lost in this veiled city and hard not to lose one's heart.

Altogether, I spent five years in Italy during which I felt rather like a surfer: sometimes under the waves, sometimes riding the crest. I loved the landscape, the architecture, my teachers and good friends, but apart from Daniele Paris, the only man who never made a pass at me, the mild irritation with Italian men grew to a full-blown allergy. Their incessant, often obscene advances became intolerable. Travelling on the night train from Rome to Messina for a concert, I was asleep in an empty compartment when five youths came in and jumped on me. I screamed at the top of my voice and the conductor came to my rescue. He took me to a first-class compartment and locked the door. I let out all my anger about Italian men. He listened sympathetically: 'Come, come, Signorina, calm down, you are in safe hands now.' I thanked him for his help. 'You see, not all Italian men are bad.' Then he moved next to me and with a cheeky smile, said: 'Give me a kiss, amore, I love you. Why don't we leave the train at the next stop and get married?' I couldn't believe my ears. I wanted to strangle him and threw him out.

There was a pompous student in my class whom I disliked as much as he did me. We never exchanged a word during our time at the Academy. A year after we graduated, I met him at a party, where we managed to avoid each other, but leaving at the same time, he offered to give me a lift home. When we got there, he suddenly bent over and tried to kiss me. 'Get off, what on earth are you doing?' I yelled. 'But I have to,' he uttered, 'if a man doesn't make an advance, the woman will be offended and won't consider him a proper man. We may not be good as friends, but we are, of course, the best lovers in the world.'

Still, I encountered many remarkable people. One whom I particularly cherished was Rosita. I actually had a boyfriend, a Bulgarian I should add, who was teaching Italian in Perugia. He was staying in Rosita's farmhouse just outside the town. It was a wonderful old stone house with a big terrace overlooking rolling hills and Perugia in the distance. Rosita, a rough peasant woman, rambled through her courtyard from dawn to dusk in a dirty apron, swearing at her turkeys and chickens in a high-pitched voice. Nobody could escape her sharp, blasphemous tongue that included all the saints she could think of, but her pasta was the best in the world, and the coffee she made in her coffeepot without a handle was to die for. She once told me the secret: 'If you want good coffee, you must never wash the pot – it must be black inside. That's why I won't replace it, I have had it since my marriage.' In spite of cursing the saints all day long, she always called a priest to bless the house at Easter. I asked why she needed him when she wasn't a believer. 'One never knows,' she beamed, 'it's better be on the safe side, just in case.' One night I was on the terrace outside my room listening to a record of Schubert's Death and the Maiden quintet. Her shutters suddenly opened above me with a loud screech and her scruffy head leant out the window: 'Rosita, I am sorry, did the music wake you up? I will stop it right away.' 'Oh no, please don't, I have never heard anything so beautiful. I don't why, but this music makes me feel that God exists.' And we listened in the dark, Rosita, propped on her elbows at the window and I below. One Easter eve, while the pious fasted before going to midnight mass, Rosita prepared a sumptuous five-course meal to celebrate with her family and invited us to join. After delicious food and many bottles of her husband's homemade wine, the evening was getting a little out of hand – jolly and noisy, drowning in laughter at the ribaldry coming from her son-in-law's foul mouth. During coffee, as a joke, we proposed to take them to the midnight mass in Assisi, sure that they would refuse. Assisi was only a short distance away but none of them had ever been. All of sudden, Rosita became dead serious and to everyone's surprise, declared she wanted to go. After the initial stupor, they all disappeared and reappeared in their best outfits, Rosita hardly recognisable in a dress and a hat. We piled into the car and drove in silence. When Assisi Cathedral came into the view, shining like a jewel on the top of the hill, they all gasped. We entered the main church with Giotto's breath-taking frescos. Then went to the lower chapel where Franciscan monks were chanting, lit by hundreds of flickering candles. The family stood with jaws dropped. They drew close together, each holding a lit candle, still and silent like devout statues. Rosita, possessed by religious fervour, went even further – she joined the queue and took Holy Communion.

Every three months, I had to have my passport extended at the Bulgarian embassy, after which I had to go the Italian police to get my resident's visa. Here I would wait for hours in the gloomy corridors and often was told to come back another time, as they were out for lunch. Eventually, the Bulgarian Embassy refused to extend my passport and threatened me. 'You have a month to pack and return, otherwise your mother will lose her job and your brother will be out of university.' The Bulgarian consul began to appear more and more frequently at my lodgings. 'Get dressed and come out, a car is waiting downstairs. We have some important people to entertain and need your help.' I realised with horror they were trying to recruit me as a spy. The more I refused, the nastier they became. I felt trapped between Bulgarian threats and Italian bureaucracy. Then the fainting began. Walking in the street, my ears would suddenly start ringing, everything would turn black and I would pass out on the pavement. Strangers would pick me up and sit me in the nearest café where I would remain for a long time before being able to continue. I felt terrified to go out and as the fainting became more frequent, a friend suggested going to her doctor, but I declined. I still hoped the consul would extend my passport but one day he snapped: 'Enough. There is nothing more I can do for you, you must go back, or find somebody and get married.' This threw me completely. It was obvious he didn't want the responsibility in case I sought asylum. The fainting continued. Finally, I gave in and went to see my friend's doctor. He asked me a few questions, took my pulse and declared: 'I don't see anything wrong with you. What you need is vitamin C and to leave Italy! Why don't you go to Switzerland?' But with an expired passport, this too was out of question. I thanked him for the advice and left, feeling wretched and miserable. The fainting continued. A piano course and competition in Taormina came to my rescue. As soon as I was on the train to Sicily the gloom somehow lifted.

There was a French pianist on course, Sebastien, a born clown so brilliant we wondered if he had chosen the right profession. Remarkably athletic, he was able to twist his body into any position and crawl under the smallest piece of furniture. We waited eagerly for his arrival at the café, walking on his hands through the traffic, or springing from underneath a table to take his seat as if nothing had happened. He used to throw a small moneybag with great panache at the waiters when paying. We named him *D'Artagnan* after one of The Three Musketeers. Before auditioning for the course scholarships, he made a bet: 'If you win, you take me dancing and vice versa. Let's shake hands on it, but don't worry, I am a notorious loser.' As it happened, we both got a scholarship and went dancing anyway. He was a fabulous dancer, so graceful and agile that I wanted just to watch and retreated to the wall, other couples following suit until he was alone, dancing as if in a trance. When the music stopped, everybody applauded. D'Artagnan ran horrified out of the hall. I found him weeping in the garden. 'I told you, I am a fool. I feel so embarrassed.' The more I praised him the louder he cried, like a child, with his head on my shoulder. We walked back in silence. I couldn't understand what had upset him so much. The next morning, D'Artagnan was entertaining the crowd as usual. And so, between fits of laughter and crying, our friendship was born.

Sebastien and me

Once the piano course ended, the competition started. Both Sebastian and I got to the final, which meant playing a concerto with orchestra. I was to play Beethoven's fourth piano concerto, which has a lengthy orchestral introduction. The piano then enters with two voices moving up the keyboard in octaves. As I reached the higher register, no sound came from my right hand. I froze, not knowing what to do. The orchestra, the jury, all eyes were on me. Finally, I got up pointing at the piano. People jumped on stage, touching the keys – there was no sound in the upper register. The session was suspended, and I was allowed to leave the stage. It turned out the lid was not placed correctly and had muted the hammers. After the tuner had corrected it, I was called back on stage, and had to start all over again. It was not my best performance, but somehow, I managed to play and was surprised to receive a prize. The competition ended with a gala concert in Taormina's magnificent Roman theatre. None of us had suitable clothes for the occasion, so we went frantically through the town looking to hire some evening wear. It was hilarious. We arrived at the theatre and sat in the warm Sicilian night under bright stars, wearing a second-hand wedding suit and dress.

Taormina is a small town, nestling at the foot of Mount Etna. On the last day, we decided to take a closer look at the volcano and, thoughtlessly wearing only summer clothes and sandals, hitchhiked to the highest point cars could go. By the time we had climbed to the only refuge, it was already late afternoon. At almost three thousand metres, it was freezing cold, but Sebastian, determined to take a photo of the crater before dark, was off, up the last ascent. I went after him shivering and slipping on the ash-covered snow. He was climbing like a goat, way too fast for me to keep up. My feet weighed a ton, and every step became an immense effort. There was also a suffocating smell of sulphur which made me dizzy. Sebastian was nearly at the top, when I slipped and fell. He kept waving at me, but I could not move. He ran down to me and gasped: 'Good God, you look green, are you OK? You must go down at once. I just want to take a photo and will catch up with you as soon as I can. Be careful – go slowly!' The descent proved even harder. After a few steps, I slid and tumbled like a stone down the slope, gaining speed as I went, until I hit a rock, cutting my leg, but at least it stopped me. The rock was hot and rough with red cinders smouldering at its base. Desperate for warmth, I propped my back against it. There was nothing to do but wait. Various scattered rocks on the ashen slope gave out a reddish glow like evil eyes fixed on me. The roar of the volcano was terrifying. If hell existed, it must be just like this – ashen, foul smelling and lethal. Relieved to see Sebastian running down, I tried to get up, but collapsed. He picked me up, propped me on his arm and we continued down painfully slowly. It was dark when we reached the refuge. The guides there were furious: 'You should never have taken such a risk. No one is allowed to go on that slope, it is far too dangerous. In order to see the crater, you must join the tour.' Pretty shaken and wounded I was still determined to see Etna erupting. We hired warm clothes and shoes from the refuge, and after a short rest joined the group leaving at midnight for a three-hour climb. On the way, we saw many holes with columns of fire frequently flaring up from the ground. We asked the guide if he could predict where these fire holes would appear. He shrugged his shoulders: 'Not really. There is no way to know. This one,' he pointed, 'appeared a week ago. It can happen anywhere and at any time, even where you are standing right now.' As we approached the crater, we were awestruck. Molten red rocks were hurled with a mighty roar high up into the sky, then would form rivers of fire flowing slowly down the volcano. Then the dawn came. It was an unforgettable experience to watch the sun rising from the sea far below us. A few years later, Etna flared up and the lava buried the refuge where we had stayed.

Back in Rome, I was plunged into the old despair. Without a passport, banned from the Embassy, I was a *persona non grata*. This desolate state felt as if it would never end. Then, one day I received a letter from Sebastian: 'I've found the perfect teacher for us in Geneva – Louis Hiltbrand. He is an extraordinary man and musician. I am sure you will like him. I've told him all about you. You must come.' Geneva? It was just as the doctor had prescribed. Then another letter arrived from Switzerland. I read it in shock and disbelief. It was from my oldest friend, Christina, whom I thought was dead. I had already mourned for two years since my parents told me both she and her father had been accused of espionage and shot after a dubious court trial. I read the letter again and again. It ended: 'I am alive and safely back in Geneva after an ordeal far too long to describe in writing. I would so love to see you and tell you the story in person. Can you come to Geneva?' These two letters stand like beacons in my mind as if Geneva itself had called me from across the Alps though I still have no idea how I managed to get there. Sebastian must have persuaded Hiltbrand to send an official invitation for me to study at the Conservatory. All I remember is that, in less than a month, I was in Geneva. A miracle.

SWITZERLAND

It is good to leave each day behind like flowing water, free of sadness.
Yesterday is gone and its tale told. Today new seeds are growing.

Rumi

As the train approached Geneva station, I paced up and down the corridor unable to keep still. What would Christina look like now? I hadn't seen her for so long. She had been allowed to study languages in Geneva, had worked there as a translator for the UN and then, the terrible silence. Yet, there she was, unmistakable, the same dear face, running along the platform with a huge smile. My heart jumped a beat. We fell into each other's arms. It was surreal kissing her warm cheek after grieving her death for so long. We cried, we laughed, then hardly stopped talking for the next forty-eight hours. Christina was pretty much alone in the world: her mother had died of cancer when she was fifteen, and then her father was shot as an enemy of the state. She now feared what might have happened to her grandmother. 'I am so worried about her,' she sighed. 'I don't even know if she's dead or alive. There is no one I can ask.' I suggested we could find out from my parents. 'Are you crazy? No way. Even mentioning my name is too dangerous. Anybody associated with my family is in trouble.' 'So, what am

I doing sitting here with such a dangerous person?' She laughed. 'Watch out – you may live to regret it.' I had to keep touching her to make sure I wasn't dreaming. She then told me her story.

It started with a call from the Bulgarian embassy. She was to go there at once. 'When I arrived, they took me to a room and introduced me to a girl waiting there. I wondered where she came from, but before I could speak to her, a man entered the room carrying a briefcase, and after a short greeting, immediately came to the point. "You are both professional translators and we need your services for the Bulgarian football team playing in Damascus. We trust you are willing to give a week of your time for your country." You know the jargon – there's no way you can refuse, it's like an order. He pulled a folder out of the briefcase and showed us the itinerary. The whole thing was planned to the last detail. I had to drop everything to go to Damascus. It was exasperating, but I had no choice. An embassy car was waiting at Damascus airport to take us to our hotel, where we were to be picked up for a tour of the city, then collected the following morning for interviews with the press at the embassy. The next morning, we were taken to the embassy, and asked to wait in a room for the television crew to arrive. There was even a tray with coffee and sweets left on the table for us. Everything seemed very well organised. Before long, a man opened the door and asked my companion to go with him and I was left alone. I was relaxed at first, but when half an hour had passed, and she was still not back, I began to suspect trouble. Suddenly, two men came in, seized my handbag and dragged me to another room with two chairs and a table. They forced me to sit, then began interrogating me. It lasted for twenty-four hours, with no food or water. They never left my side. They even took me to the toilet. "We have proof you were conspiring with your father against our country. We know you concealed microchips in books you sent him. If you confess now, it will be easier for you." They just kept repeating this over and over. 'What a nightmare, it sounds horrendous. How did you reply?' I asked. 'Of course, I protested. I am not a spy, you are mistaken, I don't even know what a microchip looks like. But they just continued stubbornly: "We have evidence. Confess, confess." My head was spinning. After grilling me for twenty-four hours, they too got tired and went into the corridor for a cigarette, leaving the door open. It was then I overheard one of them whispering to the other: "I've had enough. Leave her alone; there is not much we can do now. Anyway, the plane is coming tomorrow." At that moment I knew I was in danger. They had concocted a brilliant plan to bring me back to Sofia to stand trial for espionage with my father. The excuse of translating for a football team in Syria (with close ties to Bulgaria) was very clever. Bringing another person into the plot was brilliant – I had doubts before but was reassured when I met her at the embassy in Geneva. I had to act immediately. There was a door behind my chair, I jumped up in a flash, opened the door, and ran like mad through empty corridors and down some stairs that by chance led to the back entrance of the embassy. How nobody was there is a mystery. It all happened as if in a dream. I ran onto the street, waving frantically at taxis. I could hear my interrogators coming after me, shouting: "Stop! Or we will fire!" It was rush hour – all the taxis were taken. I kept running in a frenzy, with my pursuers getting nearer and nearer. Just as one was about to grab me, a taxi stopped. I squeezed in and shouted – Swiss embassy! Thank God, the driver understood and pressed the accelerator. He had seen the men chasing me and sped off like a demon through the busy streets. By the time we reached the Swiss embassy, he had lost them. I gestured for him to wait, and rang the bell, calling out: "Help! I need asylum, let me in!" But the concierge barred the door: "The ambassador is out, and I don't have authority to let anyone in. Come back tomorrow morning." He shut the door in my face. I ran back to the taxi, horrified to see black cars pulling up in front of the embassy. The driver saw them too, and sped off again, taking a sudden turn into a back street. Luckily, he knew the American, British and French Embassies, and we tried them all, but each refused me for the same reason – no ambassador present. I will never forget what that taxi driver did for me. Our last chance was the Italian Embassy. I rang the bell as the ambassador was coming out. Luckily, he was late for a reception. He took one look at me, saw the cars stopping in front of his embassy, and pulled me inside. "Wait here until I come back." He closed the door behind him. Shaking all over, I stood there in shock. I was safe for the moment, but not at all sure I wouldn't be thrown out on his return. Don't think, don't think, I repeated to myself. Suddenly, I remembered my driver – I never paid him! Though, how could I? I had nothing, no bag, no passport, no money, just the dress on my back. I couldn't even thank him for saving my life.'

I listened riveted by her story. 'What happened then?' 'The ambassador took me in without any questions and frankly, saved me. I must have been born under a lucky star to fall into the hands of such a remarkable man.' 'I am so grateful to him for bringing you back to me! Are you still in touch?' 'I call him regularly. He is now retired and lives in Rome. I am still unable to take in what he did for me. Each day on waking up, I thank him. I spent the next six months in a room on the top floor of the embassy. He provided everything for me, food, clothes, even a toothbrush. You can't imagine what trouble he went to because of me. The embassy was surrounded by heavily armed Bulgarian and Syrian militia, under constant surveillance the whole time I was there. I was not allowed to open my window at any time, nor be seen near it. But I could look out through a hole in the curtain. The ambassador came every day, bringing me books and sometimes chocolates, and would tell me of any progress in negotiations for my release. He would cheer me up and give me hope. But months passed and I was still living behind drawn curtains, with no sunlight or fresh air. Time passes very slowly when one is in no man's land. Sometimes I didn't know if I was dead or alive. After six months, when all legal negotiations had failed, the ambassador came up with a plan: 'I've tried everything, without success. The only way out, if you agree, is to hide you in the boot of my car, drive across the border to Jordan and put you on a plane to Geneva. It's quite dangerous, but I am willing to take the risk. The boot of the car is large, we could pad it with cushions, it won't be comfortable, but once we cross the border, you can sit in the car with me.' 'Wasn't that incredible? He risked his reputation for me. I can never thank him enough. So, here I am, alive. But they shot my dear father for nothing. They confiscated our home. I have nothing left from the past.'

It made us cry to remember the happy days we spent together in her beautiful home, giggling schoolgirls on the sofa, eating delicious cakes made by her grandmother. Later, I used to stop at Christina's if I was playing a concert, the main hall being across the street from their apartment. I would warm my frozen fingers in a bowl of hot water that her granny brought me. It was so strange to think complete strangers now lived there – a place to which she could never return. I was amazed at her courage and stamina. 'What a shocking story, why don't you give it to the press? It's a shame no one knows the truth about your father.' 'What for? It will never bring him back.' Switzerland, Christina's refuge, felt like a place of healing for me too, after the trauma of Rome. In this small country of high mountains and valleys, I felt safe for the first time. Ordered, clean and quiet, without harassment and chaos – it was just what I needed. Staying with Christina in Geneva, a city cradled in the mountains, with its grey apartment blocks, trams and winter fogs, reminded me of Sofia. It felt like home.

After a week, Sebastien took me to the Conservatoire to meet Hiltbrand. As we entered his room, the smell of cigarettes was overwhelming and it took me some time to spot him through the dense smoke, standing by the window. He looked like a statue: his leonine profile seemed carved from granite. He turned to greet me with blue, razor-sharp eyes. 'Welcome!' he said with a smile, 'take a seat.' For the next six hours I listened to him as he tormented student after student. He spoke in French, which I did not understand, but he was talking with such passion and eloquence that it needed no translation. Sebastien was right – he was the one I had been waiting for. From then on, my life was in his hands. All I wanted was his approval – nothing else mattered.

Born with a very rare congenital disease that limited his life expectancy, Hiltbrand had learnt early that each day counted. An avid reader, he was

Hiltbrand

passionate about literature, philosophy, religion, medicine, botany, art, as well as music. His house was filled with books; he would often read to me, from handwritten notes, passages that had impressed him. He did not only teach music he taught life: a powerful and dangerous teacher – exigent and exciting, challenging and encouraging, mocking and gentle at the same time. I was a bundle of nerves as soon as I entered his room, where everything was covered in ash – the keyboard, the carpet, his clothes. We students took turns to open the window, gasping for air. But in this smoky room, slowly cooked in his alchemical fire, a transformation took place. He was just as powerful when playing as when teaching. I could sense Beethoven, Bach, Schumann and Brahms hovering in the room. Because of his illness he could not have a concert career; it was Dino Lipatti who proposed Hiltbrand to take over at the Conservatoire when he himself became ill.

Hiltbrand was unpredictable; sometimes soft as a feather, sometimes so cruel and insulting, it was devastating. There is a line by Rumi – *'When you see someone beating a rug, know that the blows are not against the rug, but against the dust in it.'* Hiltbrand was relentlessly beating the dust of our egos. 'You can't become an artist without developing your Self. Playing an instrument is not enough – read, observe, feel, think. Otherwise, you will never understand the meaning of music. Don't show – be!' he would insist. 'You must abandon all that prevents you from being what you are. You must never feel reassured; that's how you become fossilised. You surround yourself with objects, old habits and concepts, and think *this is what I am*. To define yourself in that way is like preparing your tomb instead of living. Life is now. Give it all you have.' I became like clay in his hands.

Hiltbrand had many great qualities, but punctuality was not one of them. To be three hours late was as normal for him as continuing a lesson way after midnight. He had keys to the Conservatoire and could come and go as he pleased. His smoky room with two grand pianos drew me like a moth to a candle. Studying with this titan and being in Geneva was wonderful, but I did not have a piano. Every day, I had to go very early to find a room to practice in the Conservatoire before the other students came. I often spent hours sitting on a bench in the front hall, waiting for an available room. I would get home exhausted, after midnight, and tiptoe to my room not to wake Christina. There was always a note on my pillow – *I left some food for you in the fridge – EAT.* I was not hungry at that hour, but as soon as I closed the door of my room, she would appear in her dressing gown. 'Come to the kitchen at once.' She would put food on the table, open a bottle of wine and we would feast till early morning. The Swiss are very strict about noise. It was forbidden to play music or listen to the radio after ten. Even flushing the loo was a problem. But the more careful we tried to be, the clumsier we became – bumping into chairs, dropping things on the floor and unable to stop laughing. We slept little but laughed a lot, which proves that laughter is as healthy as sleep.

Geneva is a small city and it's impossible to go anywhere without running into friends. I would always find someone for a coffee and chat at our favourite café by the Conservatoire or would go with friends for a stroll around the old town or down by the lake with the white peak of Mont Blanc in the distance. Every weekend, Christina, Sebastien and I, went for a long walk out of town, then shared a plate of local fish and pommes frites in some small village by the lake, watching the sun set over the Alps. I was so happy: nobody pursued me, there was no whistling on the streets, no more threatening calls from the Embassy. I loved Geneva, the mountains, Hiltbrand and my new circle of friends. The only problem was when they wanted me to join them for a meal in France, as I had no papers to cross the border. They would hide me under a blanket on the floor in the back of the car. They found this adventure amusing and I went many times to France wrapped like a bundle of laundry. Luckily, the border police never discovered me, and the danger seemed to increase everybody's appetite – the meals were always delicious.

The Swiss are well known for being reserved, but I have never experienced such openness and generosity. Among those I met, many were wealthy music lovers and great benefactors for young students. Sebastien was supported by Madame Hat, a charming old lady, who offered her country house near Geneva for us to practice on a wonderful concert grand. She sometimes listened to the rehearsals, sitting discretely at the back of the room. She was a cultured and fascinating woman who, during her long life, had travelled the world and heard many great musicians. We would go for walks in the countryside around her house, and on returning would find her at the door in an old sweater, waiting to invite us to join her for supper. This became a routine. I still remember the aroma of her delicious soups and baked bread as we followed her into the kitchen. We sat round a large wooden table under a huge oak beam, from which hung a lamp whose warm glow shone on polished copper pots, strings of onions, peppers and garlic hanging above the stove. A glass of wine in hand, we listened to her stories – the musicians she had known, the Wagner operas she had heard at the Bayreuth Festival and about Rubinstein who had played in her house. She was so unpretentious and welcoming, we felt part of her family. These evenings were a great treat. I couldn't help but compare her with the wealthy Italians, whose homes I found so unapproachable, I couldn't ever imagine having a meal in their kitchen. The Swiss were different; they didn't display their wealth and worked even when they didn't need to. I met a couple who were pharmacists. In their modest apartment was an extraordinary collection of paintings worth millions: Monet, Degas, Picasso. They still went to work in the pharmacy every day. Madame Hat, who was too old to drive, gave the keys of her

Mercedes to Sebastien. It was an undreamed-of freedom. We could go anywhere we liked, roaming through the mountains, driving to concerts in other cities. She also gave us her opera tickets for the season, which we could never have afforded. Geneva Opera had a good reputation, and we were lucky to hear many wonderful performances, sitting in the best seats. At the première of Beethoven's Fidelio, we managed to scandalise our neighbours by laughing uncontrollably at the tenor. In prison, in chains, in the famous last aria, which Beethoven marks with four pianissimos, he screeched at the top of his voice.

Hiltbrand was becoming extremely demanding. He changed my posture, the position of my hands and fingers. For some strange reason, he was determined that I should finish the Course of Virtuosity in one year. The requirements were a huge repertoire to learn, a solo recital and concerto with Orchestra. He pushed me far beyond my limits. On top of it all, trying to understand him with my poor French often made my head spin. At lessons he would stop me after a few bars: 'What do you think you are doing? What's this blah, blah, blah? It's so boring. Wake up. You sound like a Swiss cow!' Embarrassed and humiliated, I would try again and again. Enraged, he would pace around the room, throwing insults at me until I burst into tears. 'Oh, what big crocodile tears, what a great achievement, but is this all you can do? Pull yourself together! Tears don't help, only effort. I know you can do it, try again.'

I was torn to shreds and felt so desperate I wanted to give up. I didn't touch the piano for days, but then at the next lesson, he would be full of praise. I never knew what to expect. Once, practising in a room next to the toilet in the Conservatoire, he suddenly burst in: 'So, it was you? I could hear from the bathroom some idiot practising and wanted to see who it was. I never imagined you were quite so brainless, practising like an imbecile.

What a waste of my time and yours too.' He slammed the door leaving me horrified. I didn't dare return to the class. But that evening, sweet and kind, he apologised and explained what was wrong. During those intense months before the exam, my feelings for Hiltbrand fluctuated between hate and adoration. I had become skin and bones, always in search of somewhere to practice, moving like a zombie from room to room and from house to house, anxious and unable to sleep. At times, I was so terrified of going to my lesson, I would invent any excuse, a headache, a cold, to avoid it. But sometimes, I would fly out of the lesson on wings. In the spring, to my great relief, I excelled in the first exam. Hiltbrand was thrilled. I could hardly touch the ground. We had a big celebration with Christina and Sebastien. I then had two months before the final public recital followed by a performance of Brahms' First Concerto. But, at my next lesson, Hiltbrand jumped from his chair and barred the door. 'You are not allowed in. No more lessons for you.' 'But why?' I gasped in panic. 'It's very simple. You succeeded in your exam but, as you know, with a lot of help from me. In the process, you have become too receptive, so now, until you find your own voice, you can't have any more lessons.' 'But…' I stammered, utterly confused, 'this is terrible. What am I to do?' 'You will have to find out yourself. Goodbye.' He shut the door in my face. Find my voice? How? I sat on a bench in the park, in shock. For the next weeks, I wandered like a ghost from house to house, numb and totally lost. Hiltbrand would answer my phone calls, behaving as if nothing had happened, but as soon as I asked to come for a lesson, he would simply say: 'Not yet, you are not there. I can hear it in your voice.'

Week after week I would try again but got the same answer. I continued searching for this elusive voice of mine that seemed nowhere to be found. A week before the final exam, I reached rock bottom. I happened to be at somebody's house, practicing half-heartedly just to fill time since I had decided to pull out of the exam and give up the piano altogether. It was useless to continue. I shut the lid and rested my head for a long time, staring into the void, unable to move. I was completely empty. When I opened my eyes, the room, the piano and everything else seemed to recede, swaying in a grey fog of nothingness. I tried to get up but couldn't move, as if glued to the chair. Was I going mad? Seized by panic, I felt breathless, my mouth was dry, I was shivering. *Do something, get out of this state, move!* I put my fingers on the lid and tapped the first bars of the Brahms concerto. Suddenly, I felt a surge of emotion spread over my whole body, flowing like a river over parched land. Every fibre of my being began to pulsate. I kept playing on the piano lid, yet could hear the music, vibrant and alive. Cautiously, I opened the lid and continued to play on the keys, hearing the music as if from afar: my fingers were moving, but I was not there, just listening captivated by the music. I tried all the pieces for the recital, and still *it* was there. I played on, unaware of the time, tears running down my face. When I left the house, everything, the trees, the sky, even the passing cars, looked luminous. I found a telephone box and called Hiltbrand. 'Finally, my dear!' he shouted, 'welcome to the land of the living.' He knew at once. 'I'll be delighted to see you in class.' This was the hardest and most valuable lesson in my life and showed how remarkable Hiltbrand was as a teacher. He withdrew to let me find my confidence by losing it. My final exam, recital and concert with orchestra went very well. I walked out of the Conservatoire with a diploma of virtuosity in my hands. A pianist friend called me a few days later: 'I have great news for you. A lady I know heard your performance at the Conservatoire and was impressed. When I mentioned your difficulties in finding somewhere to practise, she has offered to give you a piano.' I was speechless. How could I accept such a generous gift? 'Rejoice,' he said, 'I also got my piano in the same way and am happy to do the same for you.' Not long after, a Bösendorfer grand arrived, carried by four men puffing up the stairs to the fourth floor where I lived. I was overjoyed and rang my benefactor immediately to express my gratitude. She simply said: 'Don't thank me, do the same for someone else in need and please, never mention my name. I wish to remain anonymous.'

After graduating, I became an assistant to Hiltbrand; his pupils worked with me before playing to him. To teach talented students was both a great privilege and a learning opportunity for me. It was at this time I made an important discovery: teaching somehow gave the illusion of being able to play anything. When a student brought a piece of music I didn't know, I could play it perfectly when demonstrating how it should sound, but when they had gone, I could no longer play it. I had to learn it from scratch. This happened so many times, it made me realise that teaching gives you a false sense of confidence. It was a warning. Performing requires a very different skill. Many good teachers can't perform in public and many great performers are not good teachers. I have been taught by both, but those who inspired me most and pushed me beyond my limits were the performers.

I was enjoying my life in Geneva – teaching, playing chamber music with friends, giving concerts. Then, one day I received a sobering letter; my student visa had expired. As I was no longer studying, I could not work or stay in the country. The thought of giving up this beautiful life made me desperate. I spent many days with friends around the kitchen table, trying to find a solution. It all seemed hopeless. My passport as usual was the problem, the Swiss authorities would certainly reject me. Then Sebastien came up with a crazy idea.' Let's get married. It would solve your passport problem. What do you think?' 'Are you mad? That's ridiculous! How can I marry you?' We joked and laughed at the idea for days, until it became clear, this was the only way I could stay in Switzerland. I was deeply touched by his generous offer, but at the same time, it made me uneasy. A fictional marriage was a risky business. If the Swiss authorities found out, we could end up in prison. There were many hurdles. First, Sebastien had to ask permission from his family, which I could see was worrying him. His mother seemed clearly against the idea. Many letters went back and forth between them. This went on for weeks. She needed reassurance that by marrying her son I would never lay claim to anything of his. I had to sign various legal papers before she consented.

Just Married

Finally, all obstacles were cleared and, one winter morning, we were married in the local town hall. We had fun enacting a real marriage. We dressed for the occasion, and Christina was our witness. After the ceremony, we celebrated with a meal at a nearby restaurant. Sebastien stood up ceremoniously and read, from notes he had scribbled on a napkin, a speech as to how he expected his wife to behave. We laughed so loudly the restaurant manager came over to demand order. The 'marriage' was a remarkably happy event. It amused me to hear Christina tell her friends: 'When we three got married…' She was right; the three of us had become inseparable. We spent nearly every evening eating round the table, happy and relaxed in each other's company as if we had been together all our lives. However, once we were married, the complications began. I had to live at Sebastien's address for the sake of appearances. Once again, he astonished me with his generosity: 'You must move into my flat,' he said, 'I will leave a few personal things there in case anyone checks.' 'But where will you go?' I was alarmed. 'I have friends with a spare room, I can move to theirs.' I felt guilty. 'I am so sorry to make your life more complicated, I am afraid you'll soon begin to resent me.' He laughed and waved his hands. 'Don't worry, I will spend most of the time here with you. Everything will be OK.' Only a few intimate friends knew about the fake marriage. Having to lie constantly in public was hard for both of us. Sebastien was hugely popular: finding a plausible excuse when people phoned and he wasn't there, was challenging. It was hard to think of a good reason at seven in the morning when the secretary of the academy wanted to speak to him urgently, why he wasn't at home. Keeping track of what each of us said, to whom and when, was not an easy task as we were both absent-minded. We were always together holding hands, and then it proved difficult to convince Sebastien's girlfriends that we were only friends. When I tried to apologise for putting him in such a complicated situation, he just smiled mischievously. 'It doesn't matter, let them suffer if they want. This is the most amusing thing that has ever happened to me.'

Two months after the marriage, I came out of the French Embassy on a sunny day with a French passport and stepped into Freedom! The world looked bright gold, tasted like the most delicious ice-cream and smelt of mown grass and freshly ground coffee. An overwhelming joy rose like a wave over me. I was free for the first time in my life, free to go wherever I liked, free to travel the world. No more waiting anxiously in gloomy offices for passport extensions and visas, no more hiding, bundled in the back of a car. *Free …I am free…* I kept repeating, like a mantra. I ran dancing through the streets, with my new passport singing in my pocket. I wanted to embrace everyone, to shout at the top of my voice how wonderful it was to be free. My heart was beating so wildly, my chest felt too small to contain it. Thank you, Sebastien, thank you for giving me my freedom. I laughed like a mad woman, not caring what anybody thought. Here, and now, in Geneva, I was happier than ever before. Here, I had found my dearest friend alive, here I had my first home, a grand piano, a beloved teacher, and a wonderful 'husband'. Heads were turning, looking at me in amazement. Thank you, thank you! I even wanted to thank the Communist Party for all the trouble they gave me, as otherwise, I would never have known this ecstasy of freedom. I kept glancing at my new passport, like a diamond ring – now I was Madame Risler.

But ecstasy is fleeting. I was back to my routine of teaching and preparing concerts when the news came that my mother had to undergo an operation for cancer. It was unbearable to be so far away from her. I waited helplessly by the phone for news. The threat of losing my mother made me aware how much I relied on my parents being alive. All my achievement was meaningless if I couldn't share it with them. After an interminable month of worries, I was relieved to hear that the operation had been successful, and my mother was on the way to recovery. She even became well enough to visit me in Geneva. Christina, Sebastien and I were impatient to welcome her. We filled the apartment with flowers and prepared a special meal. I dragged them to the station hours before the train was due and I left them waiting in the car, while I ran to the platform. There she was – looking shockingly thin and fragile. I could not restrain my tears. I hugged her and it felt like holding a frightened child. We walked together to the car. My mother was as thrilled to see Christina alive as I had been a year before. They embraced and wept together. She told Christina that her grandmother was alive and well, and we wept again with joy. It was wonderful to see Christina so happy. By the time we got home my mother was exhausted. But, each day and through the weeks that followed, she got stronger. She gained weight and the colour on her face returned. Sebastien was marvellous with her; his peculiar Franglais made her laugh, and soon, she got into her teacher's mode and began correcting every word he uttered. We took her everywhere with us – drives in the countryside, to the mountains, to concerts, and to dinners with our friends. She enjoyed everything, became very popular and loved by all. The month went by so fast, I was shocked when it was time for her to leave. We drove in silence to the station. I was happy to see her looking so much better and smiling as

Mother and me in Geneva

the train pulled, out. Though, coming back to the flat and seeing her room empty was heart breaking. On the bedside table was my old cookbook which she had brought from Sofia. The memory of how it came to me made me smile.

During Stalin's regime, my mother was so fearful she would always whisper in case neighbours overheard and reported us to the secret police. Every time the bell rang, she was terrified. An early morning ring was the worst: most arrests happened at this time. A black limousine, gliding like a panther through the streets with the KGB behind dark glass, made everyone shudder. Even after Stalin, when the system relaxed a little, she couldn't get rid of her fear and went on whispering. Years later, visiting me in London, she still whispered, no matter how much I tried to convince her there was no danger. 'You never know who might be listening'.

So it was, that one summer at my parents' house by the sea, she got into a terrible state on discovering our neighbour had sold his house to the private secretary of our president Todor Zhivcov. Mother lost her peace. We couldn't talk freely anymore. 'Keep your voices down,' she would whisper, rolling her eyes anxiously towards the neighbour's terrace, 'she can hear every word!' But the secretary happened to be a lovely woman and a very good cook; she often came over for a coffee bringing a homemade cake, still warm from the oven. When a student in Italy, visiting my parents at the seaside, I mentioned to her I was looking for a Bulgarian cookbook to take back with me. She immediately went next door and brought over a book with old recipes from different regions of the country. It was beautiful. 'Where can I get this? I asked. 'I'm afraid you won't find it anywhere.' She couldn't say it was meant only for members of the Communist Party. I copied a few recipes by hand and the conversation turned to something else. Back in Sofia, the day before my departure for Italy, my mother glanced at the window and turned ashen in panic: 'My God, the black limousine is here. They are coming to arrest us. We are finished.' 'What are you talking about, who is coming?' 'Look, a black limousine just stopped in front of our house. That's it: we are done for.' I went onto the balcony just as two men got out of the car and entered our building. The doorbell rang. My mother nearly fainted. The men greeted me politely as I opened the door, then handed me a packet wrapped in brown paper. 'With all good wishes for your journey, from the Secretary.' They smiled and left. I opened it in front of my trembling mother. It was a photocopy of the wonderful cookbook, nearly a thousand pages in black and white all bound together with a blue ribbon. Her gesture was very touching, and strangely charming being delivered by the secret police. The book was too heavy to take with me at the time, so my mother had finally brought it.

Montserrat and Ramon often came to see me in Geneva. Enchanted with Sebastien they invited him to spend the summer in Mas Aranso, which then became many summers. He was such a marvellous clown, the whole family was captivated. Take a morning by the pool, children running around, diving in the water, others sunbathing and the grown-ups sitting in the shade under the trees… Suddenly, Sebastien would get up, jump over a fence into the field, mount a horse in his swimming trunks and gallop off madly. The whole company would watch him amazed. Every day he would perform a new trick – climbing a tree and swinging from the top branches, or do something wildly romantic, like going up into the mountains to spend the night alone under the stars. At breakfast they would bombard him with questions: wasn't it freezing without a tent, what did he eat? No, he did not feel cold, he forgot to bring food but did find mushrooms and ate them raw, they tasted much better uncooked, everybody should try. Their admiration grew and grew. They called him Superman of the Pyrenees. Those summers – the fragrant mountain air, crisp blue skies, mauve peaks at sunset – were unforgettable.

At night, the house was still bursting with people playing games and charades after supper, and when everybody moved to the music room Sebastien now joined me for duets, often playing until dawn.

Earlier, every summer, we were with Hiltbrand at his Music Festival in Thonon-les-Bains, on the French side of Lake Geneva. His students gathered there, from all over the world, for two weeks of master classes and concerts. Thonon-les-Bains is a beautiful place at the foot of the Alps. We pretty much camped in the local school, sleeping on small iron beds and having cold showers in the shabby washrooms, but also had great fun, picnicking in the mountains, playing football in the school grounds and giving concerts in old castles and churches, ending with feasts provided by generous sponsors. Sebastien often spoke about a singer he accompanied, how wonderful he was, always about to introduce us, but somehow it never happened. Then, one day when we were rehearsing for a concert, a tall man entered the room. He pointed at me, and turned to Sebastien with a wicked smile: 'Well, well, is this the wife you've been hiding from me?' Sebastien looked uneasy. For me, meeting this much praised friend, didn't make a big impression, apart from strikingly unruly hair, which was like a dark halo around his face. He was called John. He seemed witty and charming enough with a good singing voice, but I couldn't understand what Sebastien found so extraordinary. John lived in Geneva with his girlfriend, a Swiss singer. On returning from Thonon-les-Bains, Sebastien and I spent many evenings with them discussing, mainly in French, the merits of various singing teachers. I could hardly understand and was bored half to death.

One day, I bumped into John who invited me for a coffee. Why not? I thought. We talked for a long time, and about many things but when I asked about his family, he turned pale. 'I have been trying to escape them, that's why I'm here at the moment.' 'Escape what?' I asked. 'I want to become a singer, but they are against it. They don't think much of artists. I studied acting in London, even enjoyed touring in Rep for a year back home, but really all I wanted was to sing. I managed to study for a year in Berlin but felt obliged to leave even that. I then did economics in Canada in order to run the estate in Scotland.' *This man must be mad. He doesn't know what he wants! Acting or singing or being king of some castle?* It was hard to follow his reasoning. Why on earth would he leave Berlin if that was his dream? He did not answer. His father had died when he was three years old. He then told me that he was born forty-five minutes before his identical twin, and because of this, his grandmother, Dame Flora had made him a Macloud so he could look after the estate. He appeared to resent this a lot. Nothing made any sense to me. At first, I thought it was just a language barrier. But even later, when my French had improved, I could still not get to the bottom of the problem. Was it the grandmother or his mother, being or not being an actor or a singer? It all sounded utterly confusing. The more I tried to unravel the mystery the more my role changed from detached observer to sympathetic counsellor, even saviour – the trap into which many women fall.

GREECE AND FATE

John was becoming part of everything we did. Being unfamiliar with the song repertoire, I had the chance to explore the wonderful Lieder of Schubert, Brahms and Schumann by working with him. Later that summer, Hiltbrand was giving master classes in Sorrento, and four of us, Sebastien, a violinist, Chiara, John and I, enrolled on the course. We went full of expectation, though our first impression was shocking: the town boiling, noisy, dirty, full of tourists and cars. It felt impossible to stay there even for a day. On the spur of the moment, we decided to escape to Greece, where I had never been before. It felt like a perfect chance! Hiltbrand was furious of course and tried his best to persuade us to stay, but there was a boat crossing from Brindisi to Greece that evening. We packed our suitcases (full of music scores, evening wear and concert shoes, totally unsuitable for such a trip) and rushed to the station. On the train to Brindisi, we met two Greek boys who suggested we go to Cephalonia. 'You won't find any tourists there; it is the most beautiful island.' We reached Patra on mainland Greece the next morning. There was a boat going to Cephalonia the following day, so we had to spend the night in the most revolting hotel: bed sheets full of stains. In the morning we climbed into a charming, old-fashioned boat. Red velvet couches, shabby and worn, still remained from its past glory. In the middle, there was a wooden structure serving as a bar with a few bottles of lemonade rattling on the shelf and a small gas ring where an old man was making coffee. The boat was packed: peasants, with their belongings wrapped in blankets, goats, children, toothless old ladies all in black with baskets on their laps. They stared at us as if they had never seen foreigners before, which was probably true, and yet they opened their baskets and offered us fruit and bread. They spoke only Greek, so we just grinned, *efharisto*, thank you, the only word we knew. Patra to Cephalonia didn't look very far on the map, but after five hours at sea, we began to wonder if we were on the right boat. We passed island after island. *'Cephalonia?'* we would ask the passengers, but they just shook their heads. We were getting worried, yet there was nothing to do but wait. After eight hours, the boat landed in the capital Argostoli, and the passengers dispersed. We found ourselves alone in the empty port, as if washed onto the shore after a shipwreck. Still swaying from the motion of the boat, we sat on our suitcases and stared at stray dogs sniffing rubbish, with dust flying around us. We had no idea what to do next. There wasn't a soul to be seen. Some time passed before we saw a man riding a Vespa and ran like mad to catch him and showered him with questions. He spoke broken Italian. 'You wait me here, I back soon, you wait,' he said, and he disappeared in a cloud of dust. We waited and waited as the sun was setting. We were tired and hungry. After what seemed an eternity, he appeared drenched in sweat, smiling. 'Me find place, call friend in Athens, has house, I take if you want.' We followed him, dragging our luggage, until he stopped at an unfinished building. Proudly, he led us to a terrace overlooking the sea. There was a little wooden shed at the end, which he opened. It contained four sun beds. There was also a tap and a yellow hose. 'You stay long if want and put your things here,' he said, pointing at the cabin, 'no worry, no rob here. If hungry I take eat.' Yes, this was all we needed – water, beds and the best view of the sea. Our kind man, Spiro, was very pleased we liked the place. We left our things in the shed and followed him to a taverna. The food was delicious.

At the end of the meal, we thanked him and asked what we owed him. His eyes widened in astonishment. He looked deeply offended, like a child being unjustly smacked. 'No, oh, no! I just happy you come see my beautiful island.' We were lost for words. None of us had experienced anything like this before.

We spent four glorious days on the unfinished terrace, going to the beach, sleeping under the stars and meeting Spiro at the taverna in the evening. But we still wanted to explore the island, so the next morning we dragged our cases to the local bus. The driver gave us a pitying look while loading our suitcases onto the bus. 'Carry lot eh, need much?' There was no use explaining, so we smiled and climbed in. A very good-looking young man, he had a name to match: Adonis. 'Where you go?' he asked. 'We want to see the island.' His eyes sparkled.

'Leave bags in bus, I look after, you take little. I drop in place after three days, take to different, understand?' Our first destination was a small village. 'I come three days, wait at the stop.' Sure enough, after three days we found him standing there like a statue in front of the bus. 'Have good time, eh? Now see much better place.' Thanks to Adonis we toured the whole island which was stunningly beautiful and unspoilt. Cephalonia has survived many earthquakes, but one in 1953, destroyed nearly every house on the island, leaving only Fiscardo in the north untouched. It was to this picturesque fishing village that Adonis brought us next. We reached the little port which had a taverna perched on the edge of the sea. Everything looked like a stage set, spotlessly clean in the bright light. We sat in the taverna and ordered coffee. Nobody bothered to answer, nobody smiled. For the first time since coming to the island we felt like intruders. The old men in the taverna kept sipping their ouzo and avoided looking in our direction. We had no idea who to ask for a place to stay. After some time and many coffees, one man looked at us with an elusive smile and lifted a finger, which we took as a sign to follow him. He turned into a small street behind the port, pointed at a house and immediately disappeared. We stood in front of the gate, awkward and unsure, before entering a courtyard filled with pots of red geraniums. A young woman with huge dark eyes was sitting on a small stool peeling vegetables. She looked up at us alarmed, but Sebastien saved the day by putting his head on his hands in a sleeping position pointing at the house, which made her laugh. The house was spotlessly clean, and everything was white: tables and chairs, the lace curtains, the crochet covers on the beds. We fell in love with our beautiful landlady and Sebastien's expressive sign language amused her no end.

Every evening, as darkness fell, we witnessed a charming spectacle at the port. An old woman would appear with a ladder twice her size, prop it against a lamppost and climb wobbling like a cockroach to the top. Then she unfastened the window and lit the gas lamp. Then down the ladder, and to the next lamp until all four were lit. In the warm glow of the lamps, the taverna, the tables and people appeared like a faded photograph from the past. Fiscardo had no electricity and no other sound but the sea. Going home, just a hundred yards from the port, we would be enveloped in a velvety darkness under a canopy of stars, sparkling like diamonds in the sky.

One evening Adonis came just as we were going to bed. 'Ready, we go to Fiesta Ithaca! Big Fiesta, need shoes.' Ithaca? He wouldn't take *no* for an answer. We followed him to his boat. 'Are we going to the land of Odysseus?' Adonis looked blank, but it didn't matter, we were excited to see Ithaca. The boat was small, and the motor made strange noises as if it could expire at any moment. After a long time at sea in the dark we finally saw lights and Adonis steered the boat onto a beach and tied it to a tree. 'Now walk, long walk, Fiesta on top.' It wasn't a walk but a steep climb. We stumbled over stones and rocks in the pitch dark with no sign of life. 'Soon, soon, we there,' Adonis kept saying reassuringly. At last we got to the top and suddenly, there it was. A square, lit by coloured lanterns attached to the trees, was packed with people, at tables laden with food and wine. The air was filled with smoke from grills, musicians were playing, people were chatting, eating and drinking, children and dogs were running around, a big fiesta indeed. We followed Adonis to a table where his friends welcomed us, placing food and filling our glasses. *Yiamas,* we drank, *Yiamas* again and again – the wine was flowing, the whole square echoed with cheers and laughter. After some time, a drum announced it was time for speeches. First, the local priest took the microphone, then the mayor, followed by the village elders; they all took their time. It seemed these pompous speeches would never end, but eventually we heard *Yiama*s again, glasses were raised, and it was time to dance. They pulled the tables aside, formed a huge circle and, holding hands, danced with eyes closed, faces lit from within. We were pulled into the circle, moving and leaping with them, caught up in the music as if we had been dancing with the Greeks in Ithaca from time immemorial. Meanwhile, Adonis was walking around the circle, trying to get our attention, making signs he wanted to speak. 'I go now, but back for you.' He whispered, adding sheepishly: 'Me go meet girl. You dance, no worry, I back.' and he disappeared into the night. The fiesta on the top of Ithaca was unforgettable. The hours rolled by as quickly as the wine went down. It was long after midnight when people started to leave. We waited for some time in the square, but there was no sign of Adonis. Suddenly sober and cold, we retraced our steps to the cove where we had landed. Huddled together to keep warm, we sat on a tree trunk. Hours passed by and still no sign of Adonis. Had he forgotten us? After what seemed an eternity, we saw a faint light moving towards us. And finally, here was Adonis looking tired but with no sign of embarrassment or apology. It was already dawn when we landed in Fiskardo.

The next day Adonis took us to another part of the island, a village at the foot of a mountain. Beyond the houses we saw something looking like a castle on a rock high above the sea and decided to explore. The climb in the midday heat was harder than we expected. I remember the deafening shrill of the cicadas as we sweated up the hill, dying of thirst. Nobody thought of bringing water. But at that height, the views were breath-taking and of a blue one can only see in Greece. A blue haze shimmered over the sea, the smell of hot earth rose up from under a piercing blue sky, even the air we breathed seemed blue. What had at first appeared as a castle turned out to be a deserted village. The houses were intact, the church stood in the middle, still with the bell rope hanging. It was like walking through a ghost town. There were no animals, not even a cat left behind, just total silence. Even the cicadas seemed to have left with the inhabitants. Dry weeds rolled in the wind over abandoned gardens with withered tomatoes and shrunken grapes still hanging on the vines. Meandering through, we discovered a well, hidden under grasses and thorns, with a bucket on a cord beside it. We dropped the bucket hoping to find water. It took time before it hit the bottom and, to our delight, it came up full of ice-cold water. We drank and danced around the well like savages, pouring bucket after bucket over our heads. With skin tingling under wet clothes which then steamed in the sun, we wandered through the empty houses, passing from room to room with broken chairs, pots and pans covered in spider webs, rusty iron beds, dust and rubbish – all that remained of the people who had lived there. What made them leave this paradise? we mused, sitting on a bench under a porch. What if we forgot the world and stayed here forever? Grow vegetables and enjoy a peaceful old age. Dreaming in that ghostly village left me forever longing for the blue of Greece.

My friendship with John had deepened during our Greek adventure and back in Geneva it continued to grow. We often reminisced about Cephalonia wishing we were still there. I liked his sense of humour and was impressed by his knowledge of Russian literature, his love of poetry and passion for music. He was good looking, courteous and sensitive and, as time went by, I enjoyed his company more and more. I could sense he was falling hopelessly in love and being adored is dangerously hard to resist. That summer in Thonon-les-Bains, Hiltbrand and I were watching a magnificent sunset over the lake before a concert, when John walked past in a black evening suit and stood like a statue against the crimson sky. Hiltbrand looked at me and uttered the words that sealed my destiny. 'This is the man you should marry.' It felt inevitable that he would propose to me and that I would accept.

John wanted to go straight away to London to present me to his mother. I felt torn – the last thing I wanted was to leave Geneva, but I soon realised with growing alarm that I too was now inextricably involved. 'You have been urging me to return home and you were right. Now the time has come, and with you, all seems possible.' Encouraging him to face his family issues had clearly made an impact. But there was a constant nagging voice in my head: *are you sure that you are doing the right thing?* I would push the thought away, finding other things to distract me – my music, long walks with friends. Deep down, I did not feel ready for marriage or life in another country. As the time to leave approached, I became weighed down with fears and doubts. I would gaze out of the window at the branches swaying in the wind then take in the objects in my room – the old Persian rug on the floor, the crooked armchair in the corner, the art-deco vase on the mantelpiece – all the things that had made me feel at home for the first time and my eyes would fill with tears. Give up this? Uproot myself again when for once I felt settled and content? Begin all over again? In England?

The real problem was that to marry John, I had to divorce Sebastien. This meant dealing with lawyers and going through many unpleasant and depressing procedures. Our first meeting with the lawyer was a sobering affair. He explained that the only possible reason for divorce in our case was to prove that the marriage was unworkable because of professional jealousy and competition between us. We looked at each other mystified. There had never been even a hint of jealousy or competition between us. Having to badmouth each other and lie in front of the judge seemed an unbearable task. We had to attend two obligatory reconciliation sessions before going to court. These sessions were gruelling. The facilitator would ask endless questions, for which we didn't have answers. What exactly were we jealous about? How was it manifested? Why couldn't we find a solution? These were followed by long lectures about the meaning and importance of marriage that sounded like Calvinist sermons. It was torture. When, after two months, we arrived at the final court hearing it was even harder than we imagined. Standing in the witness box in front of the judge, declaring to tell the truth over the Bible and then speaking publicly against each other was devastating. I blotted it from my memory for years. The fictive marriage was very happy, the divorce left us both deeply traumatized.

ENGLAND

Do you know what the music is saying?
'Come, follow me and you will find the way.
Your mistakes can also lead you to the truth.'

Rumi

A few months later, my future husband and I set off from Geneva towards the shores of England in a hired white van, our luggage piled in the back. For a week we meandered through France. I loved the medieval towns with narrow cobbled streets and picturesque hotels. One morning, coming out of our hotel we saw a red rose slipped under one of the windscreen wipers. It seemed like a good omen. When we reached Rouen, we visited the Cathedral, which I knew from Monet's paintings, but nothing could compare to standing in front of the magnificent portals. John was a good guide, and we had many interests in common. He also turned out to be an excellent wine connoisseur and took me through the famous vineyards of Bordeaux and Burgundy. We tasted wines in their cellars and indulged in gourmet dinners, which was a thrilling experience. I had never travelled through France before and found everything delightful. I would have loved to stay longer in France, I was somehow not in a great hurry to reach England though once on the ferry, leaning on the railings and watching the coast

Arriving in England

of France recede, I suddenly felt carried across the water on love's wings, and was eager to see the land where my future life was to unfold. As the white cliffs of Dover came into view, John, overcome with emotion, whispered 'I am so happy to bring you here at last.' It seemed extraordinary that the country I had never desired even to visit was to become my home. My idea of England was based entirely on books. I felt grateful to visit the land of such wonderful poets and writers, to breathe the same air as Shakespeare, Jane Austen, the Brontës, Keats and Byron. In the afternoon sunshine, the luscious green countryside and white cottages with thatched roofs looked enchanting. But, as we approached London, everything changed. Even though it was midsummer, the sun disappeared behind thick cloud and there was suddenly a chill in the air. I shivered. Passing for miles through rows of run-down houses, everything looked provincial and depressing. My first taste of London was from a sandwich. How could two pieces of bread with tomato and cheese taste of absolutely nothing? It was like eating straw. Coffee and tea both tasted like dirty water. Oh, how I missed the cappuccino and delicious toasted sandwiches in Geneva. The pubs smelled of beer, smoke and terrible food, which I found repulsive. It was odd to see people crammed together like sardines, drinking pint after pint. How could anybody have a sensible conversation in such a place?

I was nervous when John took me to meet his mother, but I liked her from the moment she opened the door and relaxed when she welcomed me in French. She invited us to come back for Sunday lunch and I was happy to see her again. I gathered from John she had not been in a kitchen for most of her life, but now, in old age, living alone, she had learned to cook. When we arrived, there she was, anxious and flushed, moving clumsily around the kitchen, with three clocks on the counter set to ring at different times – one for the green peas, one for the potatoes, and another for the chicken in the oven. She fretted, glancing between the clocks and the cookbook. I had never seen anybody worry so much about a meal. It must have taken her the whole morning to arrange the table, find a suitable recipe and set the timing for each dish. It was touching. When everything was on the table, and we commented how tasty her food was, the purple hue on her cheeks began to fade. After lunch, John went to the sitting room with a newspaper while I helped her tidy up. We chatted together like old friends and I told her how I started to play the piano and she suggested that I try her Bechstein grand. It had a beautiful sound. We continued to talk for a while when suddenly, she put her hand on my shoulder and looking around anxiously, whispered: 'Ma chère fille, you seem so nice. Run away, my dear, run. I know he will hurt you like he did his previous wife.' I had known about John's first marriage ending in divorce but was shocked to hear his mother say such a thing. I wondered if I should tell John but kept silent.

After a week in London, we went back to Geneva to pack my belongings. It was here, the reality of leaving hit me forcefully. It was devastating to say good-bye to everything I loved: my little flat, the Academy, my pupils and dear friends. Goodbye to the familiar streets, the bakery where I bought my croissants, the café near the Conservatoire with its red velvet seats and round tables where I used to meet with friends. I cried and cried. Inconsolable.

What was I going to do in England, this strange and unfamiliar country? Deciding what to take, what to give away, what to throw, I sat in a fog, in front of each object unable to make any decisions. John was impatient, urging me to hurry. Sebastien tried to help, glancing at me sadly. Finally, the flat was empty. Another life buried. Like the departure from Bulgaria, leaving Geneva felt like a death. Standing in the empty flat for the last time, I felt a mourner at my grave.

Back in London, we moved to John's studio, one room with a small kitchen and bathroom in the basement of his mother's house. It was dark and claustrophobic. Our marriage was a quiet affair on a Monday morning at Chelsea Town Hall on the King's Road. Throughout the weekend, John had been on the phone to find the witnesses we needed for the ceremony. Finally, a couple of actor friends agreed to come. On the Monday morning, we were escorted into a formal room, wallpapered with red roses on a black background. It seemed more suitable for a funeral than a marriage. I stood trembling in front of a severe-looking woman in a black dress wearing a pearl necklace. She asked me to repeat the marriage vows after her. When she arrived at the phrase – *my lawful husband*, I mispronounced it as *my awful husband*. She stopped and hissed angrily at me: 'Listen carefully and repeat after me again.' John and our witnesses could hardly suppress their laughter, but with my beginner's English, I hardly understood the difference, and felt like a schoolgirl in disgrace. I had to repeat the same thing twice again before she pronounced us married. We celebrated afterwards with champagne in some restaurant in Covent Garden, which closed the following week, then took a walk in St James's Park and fed the ducks on the pond.

I fell pregnant almost immediately. We would soon need to find a larger place to live. For weeks we searched through various suburbs of London which all looked the same to me, no character or charm. I missed Geneva terribly. We finally took a flat in Battersea, which needed a lot of renovation. Expecting a baby made me happy and terrified at the same time. In unfamiliar surroundings, without my friends or my piano, I fell into a depression. Life had changed completely. We were now dealing with builders, looking for carpets, furniture and home necessities. John had to translate everything for me. The renovation was supposed to take two months, but it was eight months before we could move in. During this time my grand piano and furniture arrived from Geneva, which made the one-room studio so cramped we could hardly move. The birth was terribly long and complicated. I remember during my labour, John and the nurse were glued to the television absorbed in a cricket match as if I wasn't there. I've hated cricket ever since. But when they put my son in my arms, I could not take my eyes off him. I gazed at his tiny face and milky-blue eyes for hours. The only other person I longed to see at this moment was my mother, who unfortunately wasn't given permission to come. The phone was our only means of contact and we cried in both joy and despair.

Our new flat was still not ready, so when friends of John kindly invited us to their country house, we were very grateful. The studio now contained a double bed, a grand piano, a table, chairs and a baby cot, so there wasn't an inch left to move. Having a new-born baby, I desperately needed to be in my own home and being a guest in the house of strangers, however kind, was not easy even though it was large and comfortable with a beautiful garden and a swimming pool. It was August and the place was full of family and friends visiting for the weekends. John was in his element, fully engaged and happy to be with them. With sleepless nights of breast feeding, I could hardly keep my eyes open during the day, and at dinner would have to listen to endless conversations that I hardly understood. A few words came through. Hunt. Horse. Fox. Gun. My head hurt. Exhausted and uprooted I just wanted to be alone with my baby. The only thing that kept me going, was that we were going on to stay with Montserrat at Mas Aranso. After a month, we embarked on the long journey to Spain by car. Montserrat fell in love with our son Hugh, and he too with her – sitting on her lap beaming like an angel. Mas Aranso was filled with children of all ages who were delighted to look after Hugh. Finally, I could rest. By the autumn we were back in London, squeezed into the tiny studio. It was a few months before we could move to our new flat but at last I had a home and at last my mother came to see her grandson. Slowly I was becoming aware that family life and a musical career were not compatible. I was determined to keep playing, but often was just too exhausted to touch the piano. When Hugh was asleep, I too needed a few hours rest. Being a mother and a pianist felt like being crucified. A whole year passed before I could regain enough strength to lift the lid of the piano. If I could find someone to play with, maybe I would feel better. Then I remembered the violinist I had met on the beach in Ravenna where I had sang Mozart to sea. I had his contact all this time not knowing why. I was pleasantly surprised when he answered the phone. 'Melita, I remember you well, how wonderful you're in London now. You must come down to Cornwall in the spring. The festival I was telling you about has been going for four years. Musicians from all over the world are coming to Prussia Cove to study with Sándor Végh.'

I had once met Végh in Rome. A cellist from my chamber music class insisted that we hear his quartet playing Beethoven. 'You have never experienced anything like it.' I waited eagerly for the concert, but when they started the first movement, I couldn't believe my ears: it was all over the place and out of tune. I looked at my companion in amazement. 'Just wait, and you will see,' he whispered. And so, it was. The slow movement transported me to heaven. It felt as if Beethoven himself was playing inside me. The audience seemed in rapture, breathing with the music as one single body, until the notes faded into silence. 'You see now what I mean,' said my companion. The next movement brought us rudely down again, and then we were back to heaven. This happened throughout the whole cycle of quartets – heaven or hell with nothing in between. 'I told you he is unique. He takes great risks, but when he hits the mark, no one else touches such heights. Let's go backstage, I will present you to him. Here, the members of the quartet stood surrounded by their admirers at the four corners of the room, as far as possible from each other. After thirty years locked in a marriage together, they could hardly bear each other's company. We had to wait a long time for the big crowd around Végh to disperse before we could approach him. Struck by his vivacious blue eyes, illuminating his enormous bulldog-like face, I stood reverently, searching for words to express my admiration. Bent like a broken arrow, after a car accident had left him unable to straighten his spine, he looked at me sideways from below for a moment, and after enquiring where I was from and what instrument I played, he poked my arm with his finger: 'You are one of us. I am sure we will meet again.'

Sándor Végh

My new acquaintance from Prussia Cove suggested we play some Beethoven sonatas. How wonderful to play chamber music again. But to my horror, from the first bars of the sonata, I discovered he was not even a mediocre player, he was worse. Even his violin seemed to suffer from the awful scratching noises he drew out of it. I couldn't stop, of course, or show how I felt, so we played a whole sonata until we had thoroughly murdered Beethoven. When we finished, he was glowing with enthusiasm: 'Oh, that was so marvellous! Sorry I am a bit out of practice. Next time, I will bring a cellist so that we can play some trios.' Good God, I thought, I can't survive another killing. But beggars can't be choosers. The trio proved to be even more excruciating: only the thought of seeing Sándor Végh in the spring, and the hope of playing with real musicians kept me going.

That April I went down to Prussia Cove, with John taking care of Hugh for a few days. I arrived in the evening while everyone was at supper. I opened the door of the dining hall and saw Végh at the far end of the room deep in conversation. Suddenly, he looked up and beckoned me to his table: 'What a nice surprise,' he said, 'I remember you. We met in Rome. What are you doing here?' I mumbled that I had come to listen. 'Nonsense, you must play.' He pointed to a girl at the next table. 'She is an excellent violinist and the one next to her is a good cellist. You must play a trio together. Go now and arrange it.' I was speechless and totally unprepared but did as he commanded. The next morning, I listened captivated by the sounds coming out of his violin. His teaching was very particular – he seemed to draw the soul out of a student, infusing them with his enthusiasm and passion. Holding his Stradivarius in one hand, all flushed, with hair ruffled like the mane of a lion, waving his hands in the air, explaining in a thick Hungarian accent, singing or rather growling the melody at the student, he looked like some mythical figure gathering spirits from above. 'Look here,' he roared, 'these are not just a bunch of notes, these are the cry of a desperate mother over her dying child, you must vibrate with the heart, not just with the hand!' He would demonstrate again and again and not let go until the student got the right sound. Sometimes, he would work on a phrase for the whole morning. I was getting worried while listening, wondering if I was good enough to play for him. I felt like a child left by mistake in a room full of grown-ups, but I found each session more and more fascinating. A violinist would play a Bach Partita or a Beethoven sonata that to me sounded perfect, but Végh would interrupt the student: 'Good, good, it sounds charming, but it says nothing. Music, you see, is not always beautiful – music is a language. You cannot pack it in a box and tie it with a ribbon. Not everything is black and white, piano and forte. There are endless nuances in between. Have you noticed how the sound of your voice changes when you are happy, angry or upset? It is the same with music. You can learn to play the notes, but it is not enough. You must understand what the composer is trying to say and then find a way to convey the meaning.' He would change the bowing, the vibrato and the phrasing. 'Music lives in the silence between the notes.'

In the past, great artists often used to take talented young musicians with them on tour as a training in performance. At sixteen, Végh had joined the famous Russian bass Chaliapin, touring Europe. 'He was a fascinating man. I have never met anyone like him. From a poor peasant family he became one of the greatest singers in the world. He was a close friend of Rachmaninoff who accompanied him and dedicated many songs to him. I was very ambitious at the time and keen to hear what Chaliapin thought of my playing, so was disappointed that he never came out of his dressing room to hear me. But on the last evening, I spotted him in the wings during my performance and afterwards ran to him: "Maestro, tell me, what do you think of my playing?" Chaliapin looked at me sternly. "My dear boy, you know how to sing, but haven't yet learned how to speak. Music is a language." I felt struck as if by lightning. Ever since, my goal has been to make music speak.'

Prussia Cove was a beautiful spot. Sheep grazed on green slopes that went right to the edge of high cliffs above the sea. This pastoral idyll had a calming effect after the intensity and passion of the sessions. What made the place even more special was that music enthusiasts came from far and wide to listen and help. Once, after a morning session, I exchanged a few words with a man who worked in the kitchen washing dishes and taking the rubbish out. 'Wasn't that an inspiring session!' he exclaimed. I asked if this was his first time. 'Oh no, I come here every Easter, it's what keeps me going for the rest of the year.' Are you a musician? I asked. 'Unfortunately, not. I teach history at Oxford, but my first love is music.' In the evenings, after supper, we gathered in the music room, played musical jokes, talked and laughed late into the night, then would walk back across the fields to our cottages on the estate.

A few days later, I was to play the first movement of Brahms B minor trio with the brilliant Japanese violinist and German cellist that Végh had suggested. Unable to sleep the night before, I was so nervous that I could hardly swallow my breakfast. The room was packed with people. I watched Végh unwrapping his precious Stradivarius from its velvet cover, my hands sweaty and trembling. But when we started, my partners' playing made me forget everything. Végh's passion for the piece lifted us to a place I had never been before. It remains the most inspiring musical event in my life and marked the beginning of a long journey: how to get myself out of the way and surrender to the music. 'A musician has to become the music he plays. I am only a medium trying to transpose the vibrations of the composition, moment by moment. I let it happen to me. It's something no one can teach you.' Now, I understood why Végh's playing fluctuated so drastically. Most performers today are excellent technicians and can play perfectly even when uninspired.

But Végh was like a tightrope walker high above the ground without a safety net. He often fell but would climb up again. Sometimes, when trying to let the music happen, nothing happens. It's a dangerous thing. Végh was always looking for the spirit behind the notes: the ideal condition where the mind and the heart were united. 'Today, musicians have no ideals,' he would sigh. 'I think every person who wants to make music must have ideals. The great musicians in the past, like Furtwängler, Casals, Edwin Fischer, radiated spiritual vibration, but that has been lost. Things have become so matter of fact.' I remember one amusing session during which the players in a quartet had trouble starting together. It was fascinating to see how quickly Végh solved the problem. He asked them to face the wall and unable to see each other, they started as one. I'll never forget a very talented English violinist, with whom Végh worked intensely, changing her posture and attitude. Her playing was transformed: we were all stunned by what had happened and how deeply we were affected. Overjoyed by the result, Végh invited her to study with him in Salzburg. Sitting next to her at lunch, still excited, I said 'That was incredible! You are so lucky to have the opportunity to study with Végh.' She looked at me blankly: 'I'm not interested, I just want to work in an orchestra and buy a motorbike.' I felt as if somebody had poured a bucket of cold water over me. It was painful to see such a waste of talent.

One evening during a concert, I was watching the players on the stage, when I suddenly saw, like a vision superimposed on them, my son falling out of his cot. It was so real! I jolted from my chair and ran out frantically looking for a phone. John confirmed that Hugh had indeed fallen but luckily, was not hurt. After this he decided to come with Hugh to Prussia Cove and like me fell under the spell of Végh as did our little son. It was lovely seeing them together at lunch breaks, Hugh sitting, smiling, on Végh's knee, Végh laughing: 'Look, a cherub has landed on my lap.'

Végh told wonderful stories which were an important part of his teaching. He entertained everybody apart from his wife who had heard them many times before. Being very fond of Chinese food and hearing of an excellent Chinese restaurant in Penzance, Végh invited a few of us for a meal there. He spent a long time studying the menu most carefully as if it were a music score. He then ordered a vast selection of dishes. 'Knowing how to order is an art. Can you see how beautiful everything looks? One must match the taste with the colour; it must be good for the palate and pleasing to the eye.' Then, with the first mouthful, his eyes would roll in ecstasy. 'Oh, this is perfect. In this little morsel I can taste five thousand years of culture!' We went again the following year, where his wife interrupted him: 'Sándor, you can't count. It was five thousand years last year: now it's five thousand and one.' I went to Prussia Cove every year until Végh's death in January 1997. Some of the musicians I met there are still my dearest friends. Sándor Végh was a virtuoso violinist, profound chamber musician, inspiring teacher and revered conductor. He led his own chamber orchestra and then for many years, the Camerata Academica at the Mozarteum in Salzburg. The famous conductor Carlos Kleiber considered Végh his own conducting idol, and described him as a monster – great, wild and made of pure music. He was.

SCOTLAND

I flicker like a candle trying to hold on in the dark.
Yet, you spare me no blows and ask –
Why do you complain?

Rumi

Shortly before we were married, John took me to his ancestral home in Scotland, a journey of a thousand kilometres. Travelling through England, we first stopped in Oxford, which on that sunny afternoon looked charming. We peeped through arches into the quadrangles and gardens of the colleges, walked the narrow streets, crowded with bicycles and jolly students and admired the dreaming spires. I found the atmosphere electric. It made me envious of the students that were lucky to live and study in such beautiful surroundings. John then raced up the motorway until we reached the Lake District, where we stayed for a couple of days. I couldn't take my eyes off the glistening lakes and green hills, rising and falling like waves. We climbed to the top of a hill and looked down at stone walls crisscrossing the landscape like a patchwork quilt. The highlight for me was Wordsworth's Cottage, a picture from a fairy tale, so tiny it was hard to imagine how his large family fitted in. It had no running water, and newspapers were glued onto the bedroom walls to keep the cold out. Sitting in the garden, John read to me from a book of Wordsworth's poems that we bought there. It was a magical hour that I wished might never end.

At the border, John got out of the car and knelt on the ground with tears in his eyes. 'Isn't Scotland beautiful? Even the air smells different here.' I looked, but all I saw were flat cultivated fields stretching to the horizon with a random tree here and there that didn't seem any different from the land we had just passed through. At that moment, I met John the Scot for the first time. I couldn't see any line dividing England and Scotland, but for him, it was in the very blood. We reached Edinburgh, which I found perfectly designed, friendly and intimate. I loved the old town, climbed the cobbled streets that lead steeply up to the castle and visited wonderful art galleries. We continued our journey toward the Highlands. The scenery constantly changed. Barren moors with scattered sheep one moment, blue hills mirrored in the still waters of a loch, the next. It was dazzling. And, nowhere else had I seen the weather change so quickly. One minute a quiet sky, sunbeams staining the heather moors red, the next, vast mists and relentless rain pouring down, obscuring everything in view. Then we drove along Loch Ness, with tall trees and sheltered glens gleaming in every shade of gold. I began to understand why John loved this land so much.

Advancing further north, the terrain became increasingly bare and empty. Reaching Glencoe, the eerie landscape made me shiver. I was struck by a terrible sense of foreboding filled with ghosts from the bloody massacre of 1692 which gave the valley such notoriety. I was glad to leave that horrible place behind. We then drove west towards John's estate on the Isle of Skye. Not speaking much English at the time, when I heard the word *Estate,* meaning summer in Italian, I assumed he had a summer house there. As we approached the crossing to Skye, John became more and more emotional, bubbling with stories of battles and legends, while I listened anxious and silent. On the ferry, already tearful, he sang *Over the Sea to*

Skye. Once on the island, the sun suddenly vanished, and a low drizzle hung over everything. It seemed we had entered another world: brown sky, brown moors covered with russet heather, grey smoke curling from low stone cottages scattered here and there. Muddy paths were littered with scraps of rusted iron, old tyres and piles of peat. Not a single tree or flower, not a human being in sight. 'Where is this house of yours? Are you sure we're not going to fall off the edge of the world? How can anyone live in such wilderness? 'I asked, needing reassurance. 'Wait,' John laughed, 'you haven't seen anything yet. I must warn you there is no electricity or running water. We sleep wrapped in bearskins on stone floors. I hope you find it as romantic as I do.' We reached the end of the island. John stopped the car, put a blindfold over my eyes and took my hand. We walked for some time, then he removed it. And there it was. A huge castle, perched on a rock high above the loch, imposing and daunting. 'It has been here since the 11th century,' John told me proudly, 'withstanding the Atlantic storms and winds.' An icy hand squeezed my heart. '*Run*' it said. John continued, 'Nobody has lived here since the death of my grandmother. She was the last to have servants, cooks and maids. I am so glad that you are with me now.' Servant, cook, maid – I didn't feel very enthusiastic. 'Well,' I managed to utter, looking at the ghostly shape looming out of the rock with turrets and cannons, 'it looks… impressive'. I was terrified. Rows of windows stared back at me, hollow in the light, like blind eyes.

John led me through the back door, up crumbling stairs, past peeling walls, to the main entrance of the castle, where an enormous bull's head looked down from the top of a steep staircase. An inscription below it read '*Hold Fast.*' The damp and cold inside felt as if gloom incarnate had settled on the stony passages, the walls and the furniture, along with years of dust. A smell of decay and neglect followed us through long corridors and into rooms

Dunvegan Castle

where the eyes of ancestors watched sternly from their portraits on the walls, as if questioning why I had come to disturb their peace. John was eager to show me the castle. 'But first,' he said, 'we must say hello to the Fairy Flag.' I followed him in a daze to the drawing room. We stood reverently in front of some fragmented threadbare pieces, mounted on faded silk, behind a glass frame. 'What is so special about this?' I asked, somewhat bewildered. 'This is our most valuable possession. Nobody knows its exact origin. Some say it was a gift from the fairies to an infant chieftain. Others believe it was a farewell gift to the Chief of the clan from his fairy-lover, and its mysterious power has won us many battles.' John then told me the story of the lullaby. A beautiful fairy had once visited the infant of the Chief as he lay in his cradle. Unseen by the nurse sitting beside him, the fairy took the child on her knee and sang him a lullaby. The beautiful tune and words impressed themselves on the nurse's memory, and from then on, she lulled the child to sleep with it. It was believed the lullaby would protect the child from danger and, from then on, no nurse could take charge of the Chief's children unless she could sing it. Other stories of the clan were more alarming – countless killings, acts of revenge, wives and lovers locked in the dungeon and left to die. 'These ancestors of yours seem pretty brutal to me.' I said in dismay, as we stepped on the iron grid above the dungeon, which looked down a dark stony hole opening onto the loch. 'Many have met their death here through the centuries. A Macleod chief once invited his rival, Macdonald with his entourage, to a banquet here. After feasting for three days, he murdered them all and threw the bodies into the dungeon letting the tide wash them away.' I gave a sigh of relief as we walked outside and gazed instead at a magnificent red sky mirrored in the still waters of the Loch. It was June, when the sun barely sets in the North and here, it was almost midnight. This brightly lit world was silent, not a living creature anywhere, not a sound, not a bird. I felt as if in a dream.

The next day we toured the island in dazzling sunlight, which swept away my gloomy first impressions of the castle. Everything sparkled: the green looked greener, the sheep whiter, and the rushing cascades over the rocks were pure silver. The islands in the distance seemed to swim in liquid light. 'Where are we going?' I asked. 'It's a surprise,' said John. We walked on for an hour, climbed a hill and suddenly, below us was a white beach in the shape of a crescent moon against beautiful emerald-green water. We went down. The sand was of the finest bleached coral. I put my hand in the water, so ice cold my fingers became numb. The day of exploration ended at a wool mill, where I emerged transformed into a proper Scot – tartan skirt and cashmere pullover, ready to be presented to John's cousin Caroline, who had invited us for dinner that evening. I liked her immediately. In her seventies, she was still stunningly beautiful, with deep blue eyes in a face framed by snow-white hair. Sitting by the roaring fire in her cottage was so comforting that my fears of going back to the empty castle faded. She was an excellent cook. Through the years, the food at her table was a welcome respite after our long journeys to Skye. She and her diplomat husband had travelled widely and it was delightful to hear their stories, so different from those of the murderous clans. 'Isn't she wonderful? I am glad you liked her.' John commented on the way back, 'She has always been my greatest support. I don't know where I would be without her.' As it turned out, she became the same for me: my guardian angel.

It took me many years to get accustomed to the castle. We spent every Christmas, Easter, and part of the summer there. I don't know what I dreaded more – the fourteen-hour car journey with bored, impatient children, or the eighty steps between our bedroom and the kitchen, which I had to climb every time I needed to warm milk or bring water. John's grandmother had had an army of servants running the place, now there was only me and a freezing kitchen. I had to wait eleven years before a small bedroom was turned into a kitchen on our floor. Every time we travelled north, the car was like a grocery shop on wheels as, to my dismay, I couldn't find any fruit or vegetables on Skye (nor coffee, salad, garlic or herbs). There was just potatoes and canned food. John, who had never stepped into the kitchen before, was now delighted to invite a crowd of friends for a week to celebrate Hogmanay, with his wife as cook. Every year, I invariably ended up in bed with a fever, exhausted, unable to move. I never got to see the traditional New Year's swim, where those who dared, gulped whisky straight from the bottle and jumped into the icy loch. Hogmanay is celebrated in Scotland not only with the dancing of reels (which I loved), but then, after midnight, every house kept its doors open for the 'first footing', welcoming any stranger with a dram of whisky. Hogmanay was also an excuse for excessive drinking, a deeply rooted problem in Scotland. The persistent rain, the long dark winters and the Wee

Free Church could drive anybody to seek solace in the bottle. What else could one do after sitting through a church service for more than two hours being relentlessly condemned as a sinner? I once witnessed a funeral service that was spine chilling. I sat with the silent congregation staring at the bare coffin. Not a single flower anywhere. The preacher began the service in a subdued way, with a few words about the deceased. 'Here lies our departed, beloved husband and father, a good man, who I hope will go to heaven…' and then, like an actor pausing for maximum effect, he pointed his finger at the congregation, raised his voice and uttered a thundering, 'But… like all of you sinners, he will burn in hell forever.' I could feel a shudder passing through the pews.

To lighten the atmosphere of the castle, John and I decided to change the dull grey walls of the drawing room and ordered paint from a chart, which turned out to be a shocking orange. We waited a whole month before my second choice, a warm terracotta, arrived. John and I wobbled on ladders covered in paint for weeks to the delight of the children sticking their fingers into the pots. The house was open for tourists in the summer and our guides were bewildered by the reddish colour I had chosen, which to us, made the room warmer, though we heard rumours from the village that my artistic inclinations and communist background were responsible for the change. When we started the Music Festival a few years later and news about it reached the ears of the Wee Free Minister, I was told he had warned the congregation to keep away because *a red devil had taken possession of the castle*. How strange that on fleeing a communist dictatorship, I now found myself in a place of religious dictatorship and furthermore was denounced as a red devil infecting the island with sinful music. At the official dinner we gave for the retirement of a carpenter who had worked in the castle all his life, I happened to sit between him and the Wee Free Minister. Irritated by the patronising way the minister treated this humble, honest man, I turned towards him unable to restrain myself. 'Could you explain why you need to frighten people?' 'Fear is the only way that keeps the flock from sinning,' he replied. 'Then tell me, what is the difference between you and Hitler or Stalin? They too kept everybody in order by fear.' He looked perplexed but recovered quickly. 'I don't see the similarity. I am doing God's work, while they were Godless creatures.' Boiling, I kept challenging him. But he was adamant that the only way to obedience was fear of God. Many years later, John's funeral service was held in the Wee Free Church, the village church being too small for the crowds who came. At the door, an old man approached me, kissed my hand and said: 'You may not recognise me after so many years, but we had a conversation at the retirement of Willy, do you remember? I am also retired but am giving the funeral service for your husband and hope to do him honour. I would be very grateful if you would you pray for me.' I was stunned. How could that man whom I attacked so fiercely ask me now to pray for him? Me, the red devil, of all people? He gave a beautiful service with no mentions of hell or damnation and came afterwards, anxious to know how it had gone. 'Thank you,' I reassured him, 'it was excellent. He lit up and kissed my hand once more.

Like Willy, another favourite of mine was old Mrs Jones, the angel of the village. She had come to the island as a midwife in her youth and her small cottage was the heart of the community. I could hardly remember a time when her front room wasn't full of visitors sitting by the fire, while she ran to and fro, refilling the kettle for more tea. It was enough to see her innocent, smiling eyes to make me happy. An excellent listener, her calm and luminous gaze seemed to disperse every worry; not surprisingly people flocked to her house. After all, she had brought most of them into the world. I have never been a tea lover, but her tea was so delicious, I couldn't resist cup after cup.

Every day, regardless of the weather, I would walk the mile to her cottage pushing the pram, first with Hugh then later with our baby daughter Elena. We would listen to her stories; how she would walk through howling winds sometimes in the dead of night to deliver a baby at the other end of the isle, later going by donkey, then by bicycle. 'It become easier with a car, but unfortunately, that was only a few years before I retired.' I felt humbled by this brave lady. She was a great help and solace for me in trying times.

John had employed a caretaker, Duncan, a half-deaf retired teacher, who never heard the doorbell and wouldn't have noticed if an army invaded the castle, but he was a kind man. I did enjoy the impromptu meals I shared in the kitchen with Duncan and our cleaner Frida. She had never been to a dentist and was already toothless in her thirties. She would hold her hand in front of her mouth, which did not stop her from spouting the most notorious gossip. Nothing escaped her watchful eyes and her sharp tongue spared no one. She knew the secret love affairs, betrayals, and dramas of the whole community. Like a local radio station, she was a living history and endless source of information. There wasn't a dull moment with her. Things would often go missing, though when I asked her about an item, it would magically reappear. Poor Frida, I later understood why she had taken so many cleaning jobs. She was the only breadwinner of the family. Her husband, good-looking and an alcoholic, cared nothing about her or their children and on top, had a mistress in the village. Frida looked like a witch, but my children adored her. She had a big box of sweets and let them eat as much as they wanted. To them she was always the good fairy. Another inheritance from the past was Charlie, the old butler, long retired who lived in a cottage on the estate with his wife, Rosa. A hopeless drunkard with purple cheeks, he had a habit of sneaking into the castle for a drink. Often when I opened the pantry door, I would find him there, gulping whisky straight from the bottle and would jump with fright. He would restore the level of whisky by adding water, which meant that John offered our guests something nearer to weak tea. When Charlie's wife had a stroke, she spent several months in a coma at the local hospital. Finally, the doctors could do no more for her, so Charlie took her home, where she lay in bed neither dead nor alive. It didn't seem to bother him at all. 'She doesn't move, so I jump over her to the other side of the bed and go to sleep.' To everybody's astonishment, she recovered and returned to the land of the living. 'Rosa, do you remember anything of that time?' I asked. 'Not much,' she answered, 'I was away with the fairies.'

Another Charlie was a witty and entertaining Etonian, an old school friend of John's. He was a professional designer, now in charge of the clan archives and displays of historical objects for the public visiting the castle. He came with his family every year to celebrate Hogmanay to the delight of all. We would gather in the drawing room in high spirits after dinner, glasses filled, ready to welcome the New Year. Charlie would appear with a fiddle under his arm, his long hair tossed over the high collar of a tartan coat he had designed, looking like a Scottish version of Paganini. We pushed the furniture against the wall and formed dancing circles. He took his violin, lifted his bow in the air with great élan and the dancing began. He played reel after reel throughout the night. In the early hours of the morning, we would go down to the kitchen, hungry and exhausted, gobble the cold leftovers of turkey and potatoes and continue to dance around the table. During those short, dark days, we dispelled the gloom by sitting round the fire, playing games and telling stories, as the windows rattled. The ghosts were particularly lively in the dark, moving around with the wind at night. Nobody was brave enough to leave the warm library and face the shadows in the long corridors. One New Year, Charlie's daughter was terrified by an apparition in the middle of the night. A figure with long pale hair, dressed in a white gown, was dragging something along the floor. The next morning all became clear. The ghost she saw was John's sister-in-law, taking her mattress and pillow to the bathroom. She and her husband hadn't shared a bedroom for years, and put together when they visited us, she found the bathtub more congenial.

Charlie became the most precious friend, the only person who seemed to understand my dilemma of being torn between two worlds – wife and artist. One evening, sitting together in the library, watching the flames in the fireplace, he suddenly turned to me. 'My dear, I think it's high time you realised something, and the sooner the better. Having a talent is a responsibility that only you can carry. Do not expect help from anyone.' His words struck me like a bolt of lightning. He got up, put a log on the fire and emptied the ash of his pipe. 'I hope you understand what I am trying to say. There is nothing more to add.' He wished me good night and left the room. I stayed behind lost in thought. I had fallen into a deep hole and Charlie stretched out a hand to pull me up. Looking at the flames, a new awareness emerged. I had been trying to mould myself into something I was not and at the same time, asking 'What have I done to deserve this,' instead of 'What could I do to be myself?'

Soon after this revelation, we received an invitation to attend a Ceilidh and spend the weekend at Inveraray Castle with the Duke of Argyll, an old friend of John's. Gaelic singing and bagpipes: I couldn't imagine worse torture. And I would know no-one there. 'You go,' I said to John, 'I'll stay here with the children as I am not in a party mood.' John insisted which led to a big argument. I rang Charlie, horribly upset. He laughed. 'The Duke won't eat you up; he is easy-going and very friendly. Go, you'll find it very enjoyable. Just be yourself.' I kept repeating *be yourself* like a mantra all the way to Inveraray. The huge castle was filled with antiques and priceless paintings.

The Duke and Duchess welcomed us warmly in the vast Entrance Hall (with the highest ceiling in Scotland), surrounded by a huge array of weaponry on the walls. When we were shown to our room, I was taken aback to see my suitcase already unpacked by a maid, and my few dresses hung neatly in the cupboard, including my nightdress, which she must have mistaken for an evening gown. I found it intrusive that somebody had handled my belongings and wondered why the aristocracy had adopted customs that made them so dependent and impersonal at the same time. The Ceilidh was a challenge for my ears: the songs too sugary, the bagpipes too loud, and the crowd perspiring with an excitement I could not share. It was exhausting. I could hardly wait for it to end and go to bed. Finally we slept, but at seven in the morning, were woken by the piercing squeal of a bagpipe. I buried my head under the pillow. After half an hour the horrible sound ceased. Relieved, I put my head on the pillow for a little snooze, when, without knocking, a maid came into the room with our breakfast. She drew the curtains open and placed a tray on each of our laps. A nauseating smell filled the room. Smoked kippers. I turned to John in disbelief, but he seemed delighted. 'Hmm, kippers, a perfect Scottish breakfast and the best way was to start the day, don't you think?' Stunned by the invasion of bagpipes and smelly fish, I lost my appetite entirely.

The next evening was equally unsettling. Dinner was held at an intimidating table decorated with exquisite silver boats and lit by massive candelabras. Liveried footmen in white gloves circulated silently behind us. It felt horribly stiff, and the conversations seemed empty of any real meaning. I then remembered Charlie's advice – *be yourself*. I leant towards the Duke on my right and fired the question. 'Do people always talk such nonsense at dinner?' Surprised, he beamed at me and took my hand. 'Yes, my dear, you are right, all this talk is pure nonsense.' Then to my embarrassment, he lifted his glass and addressed the company. 'My friend here,' he pointed at me, 'has complained that we talk nonsense, and I agree.' Suddenly, the mood changed. The conversation deepened and turned to real concerns about the human condition – loneliness, fear, survival. I couldn't believe what was happening and was immensely relieved that my insolent question, which could have ruined the reputation of my husband, was so gracefully received by the Duke, who seemed to enjoy the evening as much as I did. Beneath the veneer of politeness, we were all the same. On the way back to Dunvegan I called Charlie to thank him for his wonderful advice.

The library in the castle was my refuge during the winter. I grew very fond of the long nights. By three in the afternoon, one could already see stars in the sky. I found this mysterious, velvety darkness very soothing, it made me feel like a bear hibernating. I would sit in the library by the crackling fire, the cold stars peeping through the window, a sketchpad or book on my lap. I loved the peace and would stay there until the early morning hours staring at the dying embers. It was during one of these nights that the memory of my uncle's studio came back to me. It was so vivid and real, I could see myself as a young girl, sitting behind him, intoxicated by the odour of oil paint and turpentine. This moment rekindled my childhood passion for painting and opened my eyes to the mysterious beauty of the island over which the constantly changing light would reveal the brow of a hill for a second then wipe it out with a brush of white mist. I became a light-chaser, watching it move through the drifting clouds, that revealed a blue patch of sky or swiftly covered it with dark-purple. A shaft of sunshine would touch down on a field lifting a myriad of greens from the ground. It was impossible to capture this ethereal light. It expired mid-air between the brush and the canvas.

After long months under a thick blanket of darkness, just before Easter this would lift and the whole island sparkle. It seemed like all living creatures hiding under rocks or in burrows, crawled out into the blinding light. The arrival of spring was something not short of a miracle – seals sunbathing on the rocks, sheep drying their soaked fleeces in the middle of the roads with their new-born lambs sleeping on the top of them. The islanders would smile and greet each other joyously – joy all the way from the muddy ground to the sky. One such bright day, I went down to the sea and found a beautiful spot to paint, though it was exposed to a biting wind. There was a rock above me with a nook just big enough for me to squeeze in, a sketch pad on my knees, paint box and water jar balancing on the edge. Snuggled there, the sun on my face, I became absorbed in painting. After some time, I heard the sound of splashing and looked down. An otter was in the water below, holding a fish in its paws. It looked at me for a second then dived under the surface. Astonished to witness this fiercely shy creature fishing just a few metres from me, I watched it swish gracefully in and out of the water until it vanished into the depths. I waited for a while hoping to see it again, then went back to my painting. Suddenly, another splash and the otter was right in my lap. In a panic, I sprang to my feet. The otter leapt back into the water taking with it my sketchpad, brushes and paints. No matter, it was thrilling to have this close encounter with such a wild animal. Later, I realised the nook must have been the otter's private resting spot, the price of intruding being the loss of my paints to the sea.

Observing nature more attentively changed my attitude to Skye. It revealed secrets previously hidden from my eyes, though the unpredictable weather, bringing long spells of thick mist or horizontal rain, often dampened this new-born enthusiasm. Still, I persevered, and soon had enough paintings to hang in a small turret which was open to the public. I was both surprised and delighted when a visitor bought one of them. Then, others sold. Luckily, there were a couple of artists living on the island who had turned their barn into a gallery. They showed me how to cut mounts and frame paintings. I was glad for any excuse to spend time in their company and would leave their gallery inspired, with a fresh supply of paints and paper. My first exhibition was held in the North Room of the castle, reached by a passage over the dungeon. It was both icy and forbidding but also large, with a window looking over the loch and far islands. It had the best view of the often-spectacular sunsets. We invited a designer friend from London to help with the display. He arranged and rearranged the paintings, moving them around for an entire week, but when everything was in place, the result of his painstaking method was impressive. We first invited the staff working in the castle to come and see it. I will never forget their faces. Overwhelmed by the transformation they stopped at the door. 'The ghosts have left,' they said, as one.

Buildings surely retain something of their former inhabitants. Otherwise, how to explain why some rooms have a disturbing effect while others are pleasant and welcoming. I felt a definite chill and my stomach would knot, every time I found myself near the dungeon, though in general, I was not much troubled by the ghosts in the castle. Years before my exhibition, Charlie had come to catalogue and arrange objects on display in the North Room. He had to pass through the drawing room where I was practising. I got used to his coming and going, so when my eye caught sight of a pair of feet in faded slippers standing by the piano, I assumed Charlie wanted something. I looked up, but nobody was there. The slippers vanished. I continued playing, somewhat amused that a benevolent ghost might be fond of music and had come to listen.

A different ghost disturbed us one New Year's Eve when John was away for a funeral. Sebastien was among the guests around the dining room table. He suddenly lifted his hand: 'Shh… listen, did you hear a noise? There is somebody behind the door. I can heard steps, listen… I am sure.'

It's incredible how quickly paranoia takes hold; everybody was glancing anxiously around. In the silence that followed we could hear many things; strange bangs, steps, rattling windows. All the noises no one noticed during the day, now sounded terrifying. Sebastien leapt up. 'I will fetch John's rifle. I know where he keeps it.' Like lunatics, we left the table and followed him to the gunroom. Holding the empty rifle, reminding me of Peter Sellers as a crazed Inspector Clouseau, he led us like a flock of sheep, gun in one hand a candle in the other, along the dark corridors. We were laughing hysterically, enough to scare off any ghost.

Having a castle, whatever the stories and romance, is a heavy responsibility, but it also has the advantage of hosting many friends and meeting new ones. One special occasion I will never forget, was when John received a letter from the Japanese Embassy which stated most politely that the Crown Prince Naruhito of Japan, currently on a tour of the Hebrides, had expressed an interest to visit various Scottish castles and asked if we were agreeable to hosting a dinner for him. As a footnote they added that he was travelling with an entourage of ten. John found the idea charming, while I was seriously alarmed. How could we receive royalty in this shabby place? Who would cook the dinner? We argued for days. In the end Cousin Caroline came to our rescue offering to help arrange the dinner in the best way possible. I decided not to pretend, and let the Prince taste our humble castle life, which meant walking up the stairs to the second floor, along a corridor with a tattered black linoleum full of holes, through the kitchen into our small dining room, where the chairs wobbled, and occasionally collapsed without warning. Preparations took days of frantic activity. Shopping, cleaning, polishing the silver, turning the cupboards upside down in search of matching dinner plates, wine glasses, water glasses, side plates, dessert plates and cutlery. Everybody got very excited especially Frida, but I had never felt so worried about a meal. It was nerve-racking. I don't know what I would have done without Caroline, who as an ambassador's wife was a charming and elegant hostess. But, the moment we met Naruhito at the door, his unpretentious and natural demeanour put me immediately at ease. He seemed like an old friend. During the tour of the castle, he charmed the children with funny stories, was curious about every little detail and was an attentive listener. The piano in the drawing room sealed our friendship – he happened to love music. He had first played the violin, then switched to viola, as he found the violin too showy for his taste. From this moment on everything flowed smoothly. Passing through the kitchen, he lowered his nose to the chicken casserole I had made. 'Hmm, it smells good.' The dinner was a great success (and none of the chairs broke). Courteous and relaxed, the prince enjoyed everything, and even offered to take his plate back to the kitchen. Tiny and delicate in stature, his face emanated such warmth, kindness, and intelligence that we were enchanted. After dinner we had coffee in the drawing room. I played some Bach and Beethoven for him and he expressed regret at not having his viola to join in the music. It was a wonderful evening that went by far too fast, and we all were sad to part company.

In the summer of 1970, John and I still were preparing for our annual visit to Hiltbrand's festival in Thonon-les-Bains. I was to accompany John singing lieder, as well as rehearsing Brahms and Beethoven trios with my colleagues in London. Suddenly we got the news that Hiltbrand was ill, and the festival cancelled. We all felt nine months pregnant, unable to deliver our musical babies and looked desperately for somewhere to give birth. Then, John turn to me 'Let's take it to Dunvegan.' At first, the idea seemed mad. I had yet to meet anyone on Skye remotely interested in classical music. But with no other option, we decided to try. So John and I, the violinist and the cellist, squeezed into the car with the cello on the front seat, and started the long journey North. When we got to the castle, we had to think immediately about publicity – none of us had experience in the matter. We had no printer, so I wrote posters by hand, which we pinned up in the local grocery shop and hotel. I also wrote out the concert programmes for the evening. My hand was aching by the end. When the day came, I had a panic attack – what a stupid idea, why did I drag my poor musician friends here? We were mad. To calm down I went for a walk by the sea. The concert was to be at nine in the evening. The sun was still high in the sky. Everything looked surreal in the bright light. The sea shimmered as if lit from within, the far islands glowing a brilliant green. The only living things I could see were the sheep grazing on the hills. There will be nobody at the concert, I thought as I walked back, maybe just a sheep, if we are lucky.

Meanwhile, the musicians had arranged the chairs in the drawing room. Cousin Caroline, who had brought a vase of flowers from her garden, was already sitting in the front row. Tense and anxious, we returned to the library to wait. Not a sound, only blinding sunlight streaming into the room. Nobody spoke. Then, a miracle. Steps. People climbing the stairs. More people. And more. They kept coming. John had to run frantically to bring more chairs from the bedrooms upstairs. We couldn't believe our eyes when we entered the room. It was packed. The concert was a huge success, and all the more so for being completely unexpected. People kept applauding, asking for more. Where this enthusiastic public had come from was a mystery. We had no encore, so repeated a movement from the Brahms trio we had just played. They wanted more. We played another movement. It was nearly midnight before they left. Overjoyed and relieved, we pushed the chairs to the walls and danced as if possessed. That improvised concert was the start of the Dunvegan Chamber Music Festival, which happened every July for the next ten years.

The musicians who came to play at the festival were so enchanted with the Skye scenery that rehearsing was the last thing on their minds. After breakfast they would disappear. Some went for walks, some went to an old weaver in the village to buy tweeds, others ventured to the main town for whisky, cashmere jumpers and shortbread. 'Don't worry, we will be back soon and can rehearse later.' I was very upset at the beginning and found it was hopeless trying to persuade them with words. The only thing was to start practising myself and gradually the message got though: they felt obliged to join me. The festival lasted two weeks. Having four concerts a week with different programmes was hard enough, but the late dinners lasting till early morning meant late breakfast lasting till midday. Then there was lunch and the whole day was gone. We had to house and feed everybody – musicians, children, guests, as well as rehearsing and performing. It was exhilarating, but exhausting. I could hardly stand up by the end, but it was always worth the effort. I was often advised by well-wishers to include Scottish music in the programmes. 'What do you prefer', I would ask, 'bagpipes and fiddles or music?' Each year we presented the great classics: trios, sonatas, and quartets by Beethoven, Brahms, Schumann, Rachmaninov, Scriabin and Shostakovich. It proved to be right; people recognise good music when they hear it. I remember a couple from Glasgow who became regular visitors to the Festival. They wrote to thank us: *We've avoided classical music like the plague before and never thought we would enjoy it so much. It didn't seem like something for us, but thanks to your festival we now go regularly to concerts and are immensely grateful.* The Wee-Free Church was predictably against the festival and prevented many locals from attending. Lillian, an English lady working at the ticket desk, told us how much she enjoyed hearing us rehearse upstairs, so we invited her to come to the concert. 'I wish I could, but my husband is a member of the Wee Free and wouldn't allow it.' We offered to play just for her. She came upstairs and sat on the edge of her seat, eyes shut, a beatific smile on her face. Afterwards, she thanked us every time we passed by her desk. Making a sin out of music and forcing people to read nothing but the Bible, was baffling to me. No wonder so many found consolation in whisky.

As the festival grew, Rosemary came to help with the cooking. She looked like a fairy with long, blonde braids and innocent blue eyes. We christened her Rapunzel. She was a weaver and had come to Skye with her boyfriend during the hippie sixties, settling in a remote cottage. One day, he went to the village for some errands and never returned. It must have been a tremendous shock for her. She was left alone in their tiny white cottage, on a headland high above the ocean exposed to the fearsome Atlantic winds. To reach it you had to pass through the most rugged part of the island, treeless and poor, littered with dumped rubbish. And yet, you arrived to find a magical garden – flowers everywhere, blue irises, geraniums, climbing roses, fruit trees, strawberries and raspberries, and rows of lettuces and herbs. It was like stepping into a fairyland. How did she, so small and fragile, manage to create this paradise all alone? The colours of her garden spilt into the cottage and were woven into her rugs which were displayed on the walls and covered the upright piano. There were stacks of hand-dyed wool by the old loom, and the shelves above the woodstove were filled with jars of home-made jam from the fruits of her garden. I used to bring the musicians to her for tea, to taste her delicious scones and strawberry jam, hoping they would buy a rug, which they often did, to her delight. Everybody who met her was impressed by her courage living alone at the end of the world. I saw her many years later at John's funeral, looking much the same, though her braids had turned silver. But she was still smiling. 'I miss you and the festival terribly,' she whispered as we embraced, 'the thought of it kept me going through the long dark winters.'

Musicians living together often become like naughty schoolchildren, and practical jokes became an obsession during the festival. It was impossible to guess what would happen after the concerts. Once, a big salmon with a tiny fish hanging out of its mouth appeared at the dinner table covered in seaweed, playing Schubert's Trout Quintet. They had hidden a tape recorder under the plate to present a musical fish dish. Nobody knew what to expect; you could find a billiard table leg in your bed or a bucket of water pouring over your head when you opened your bedroom door. One morning John came rushing into the kitchen, breathless with excitement. 'I just received a call from a tour operator in Portree requesting forty tickets for a Japanese group tonight. I said yes, but with so many bookings already, I have no idea where to put them. We don't have enough chairs.' He ran like a headless chicken around the castle bringing all the chairs he could find, counting them and rearranging the room, but still, there were not enough to accommodate the group. 'I will go to the hotel and ask if we can borrow some.' He fretted the whole day and even asked some guides to come and help with the expected crowd in the evening. We waited for the Japanese group to arrive, but they never materialized. That was a joke too far. Still, despite the time wasted on practical jokes and fun, the level of playing was excellent. There was only one problem: we had to keep the windows shut because of the invasion of bats and midges which often created havoc. One could never really relax on Skye – if the rain stopped and the sun appeared, swarms of midges invaded and ruined everything except the magnificent sunsets, the crowning jewels of summer, which would splash the concert room with golden-red hues, lasting to the end of the performance.

I lived in a castle with a handsome husband and two beautiful children: a fairy tale, what more could I want? But, walking over the peaty bogs in this land of swelling mists, I felt more and more lost, wondering why destiny had brought me here. I kept smiling and doing what everybody expected of me, but at the same time, I was gradually sinking into despair. The more people I met, the more houses I visited, the lonelier I felt. It wasn't anybody's fault, people were kind and hospitable, but I felt dead inside. Conversations were either about keeping the roof from falling in, or the damp from rising, or shooting anything that flew in the air or ran on the estate which was followed by endless discussions of how long the game should hang before roasting. It was like being on a diet of porridge for breakfast, lunch and dinner. I often wanted to scream – *let me out*! Remembering the life I had left behind in Geneva increased my misery. 'We hear that you used to play the piano, Melita. It must be a pleasant pastime.' What could I say? I felt demolished. In the stately homes I frequented, there were plenty of beautiful antiques, paintings and magnificent, leather-bound books in libraries, gathering the dust of centuries. I wondered if their owners had read any of them. It was also shocking to me that so few had any idea about European history or literature. Even in communist Bulgaria we studied English, French, German, Spanish, both history and literature. Here, when I mentioned authors like Zola, Stendhal, Thomas Mann, Dostoevsky, or my beloved Stefan Zweig, I received blank looks. The aristocracy had one thing in common with the working class, a deeply rooted mistrust of art and artists, discouraging their children from such unprofitable careers. John was one such victim.

The years passed quickly as we moved between London and Skye, juggling with children, schools, half terms, holidays. On top of this, I was still travelling for concerts, preparing and rehearsing the festival programmes, painting and organizing exhibitions. Even thinking about it now makes me tired. Absorbed in these activities, I didn't notice the cracks emerging in our marriage. I lived with the illusion that John was supportive, encouraging me to carry on with my career, willing to take care of the children when I travelled abroad for concerts, and I was grateful. But I began to notice that on my return, he was increasingly silent and moody. Every time a concert came up, I would ask: 'Are you sure you don't mind me going?' The answer was always, *of course, you must go, I don't mind.* In the beginning, he used to take me to the airport, but later, he didn't even get up to say goodbye at the door. I couldn't understand how he could be so encouraging and resentful at the same time – it was confusing. His resentment also became apparent during the festival. He complained that I rehearsed much more with the others and not enough with him. He grumbled about the programmes and the people I invited. The clashes increased. As the gap between what he said and did intensified, I felt I was the cause of it all. We also quarrelled about the children's upbringing and education. I was becoming more and more depressed. In London one day, I found myself sobbing in the street when I bumped into an old friend of John's. 'My dear, what's happened? Why are you so upset?' When I told her a little bit about the situation, she took me in her arms. 'This is awful. It seems John is projecting all his problems on you, and I think you need help. You can't cope otherwise.' She handed me a number. That lucky encounter changed my life. The number she gave me was that of her Jungian analyst, who also happened to be a musician. A deep connection and trust developed between us through the weekly hour I spent with him. It became my anchor. I began to read Jung and eventually acquired the entire collection of his works. He became a living presence in my life: I could hear his voice rising from the page, talking directly to me, confirming thoughts and feelings I couldn't express myself. Jung writes that our first phase of life – survival, is not very different from that of animals – homemaking, procreating and looking after offspring. After this, the road splits in two: one leads to development, the other repeats the same patterns until death. At this juncture, Jung says, to become fully human, we need to attend to what he called the University of Spirit. My re-education had begun.

At first, John encouraged my going to analysis, but as I began to progress, he became more resentful and distant. Sometimes, he would listen attentively to my reports and I felt hopeful our connection could be restored. But the next day, he would retreat into his shell, unreachable. I suggested that he too should find help, but he was adamant. 'I am fine. I don't need anything.' One evening during a heated argument, I suddenly heard myself speaking my mother's words. The realization stopped me in my tracks: my thoughts were not my own. They came from family, teachers, friends, books. It was an obvious but sobering discovery and made me listen more carefully to what I said. It didn't prevent me from repeating old habits, but at least I was becoming more aware. My analyst was a great support, and I was devastated when he told me he was moving to Zurich to take up a teaching post. 'You can put me in your pocket,' he said at our last session, 'we will continue our conversations from there! You have learned enough to continue the work by yourself.' However, while I was moving forward, John was not. When couples do not develop at the same pace, the split becomes inevitable. By our tenth summer festival, we were profoundly unhappy, even though a record number of people came for the concerts. Instead of turning them away we left the doors open, so they could listen from the stairs and corridors. It was to be the last festival.

That same autumn, I went to Sofia to celebrate my mother's seventieth birthday. She looked so young and beautiful and was glad to have her family around. She said how much she would love to hear me playing a concert in Sofia. When our friend Alipi, the conductor, came for tea, we made plans for a tour of Bulgaria in the spring. My mother was thrilled, looking forward to the concerts. We said goodbye at the airport and her joyous, radiant face is etched in my heart. It was the last time I saw her. Back in London, I fell into a black hole, hardly capable of doing a thing, except sitting on the sofa, listening again and again to the Mozart Requiem or Bach's Passions, overcome by sadness. In December, just as we were about to leave the house to go to Skye for Christmas, the phone rang. I picked it up and could hardly recognize my father's voice. Choking with tears, he told me that my mother had been taken to hospital for an emergency operation. I froze. Hearing him crying on the phone, I realized her life must be seriously in danger. 'The operation is tomorrow,' he managed to whisper. 'Come if you can, but if you can't, be here when she comes out.' Then the line went dead. I stood in the hallway in shock, my world collapsed. The children were impatient to go to Skye, and the car was already packed. The next hours were terrible, the children sobbing and John pressing me to make a decision. I spent hours on the phone to my father and then my brother, who finally convinced me to go to Skye. 'You know the rules in Bulgaria. No one is allowed to visit patients in emergency. I am here. You will be needed when she comes home after the operation.' The fourteen-hour journey to Skye was horrendous. I felt torn to pieces. The further we went, the more strongly I felt pulled back to my mother and couldn't stop the tears. That Christmas was the most miserable in my life. Everything felt heavy, like wading through black treacle. Decorating the tree, cooking the Christmas dinner, pretending for the children's sake that everything was OK, was torture. I spent the rest of the time on the phone to Sofia. I was told the operation was successful, but I couldn't calm down, expecting the worst. Two days later my brother called: my mother had died. I was alone with Hugh, who tried so sweetly to console me, stroking my hand and hugging me. John had gone for a walk with Elena. When they returned and heard the news, he simply said: 'I am sorry she died, but it is your problem. Life must go on.' Then he left the room. The words were spoken so coldly: no hug, no warmth. We were as far apart as I was from my mother, our love as dead as she now was. I felt totally alone. On that night a terrific storm hit the island, fierce winds shook the castle, the shutters banging, the curtains flying. The violent gusts blew the ferryboat three hours down the coast. There was no way in or out of the island. Imprisoned in the castle for a week, I could not get to my mother's funeral, instead I was obliged to attend a big new year's party of which I have no recollection except bleakness and absence. I had no more tears left.

Two weeks later, I arrived in Sofia to find my father inconsolable. In his grief he had made a full-size portrait of my mother from a photo. He had put it on a shelf with flowers and candles in front. 'Flowers now?' I teased him, 'how come you never gave her flowers when she was alive?' 'I *always* gave her flowers,' he grumbled. They must have been invisible. It was endearing to see him now, putting fresh flowers by her portrait every day. He had even arranged a memorial service for her and hired a choir, which he recorded and played to me every time I visited, until his death. It was strange to sleep in my mother's bed seeing her image opposite me in the flickering candlelight. Even so, it was way less distressing than the loneliness of Skye. Being at home, grieving with my family, crying and laughing, talking about her, looking at old photographs, was immensely soothing. The thought of returning to England kept me awake at night, gasping for breath, as if being buried under an avalanche. At the airport, my father held me tight, sobbing: 'I don't think I will see you again, be brave. Good luck.' This happened for the next eight years.

Arriving back home felt like landing at the North Pole without a coat. John was distant, the children were very needy, and I had nothing left to give. The months that followed were desolate and bleak. Then, one day, John announced that he was moving out. I was preparing for the Spring concerts my mother had so wanted and could no longer hear. That May I gave a recital in Sofia and played Beethoven's Fourth Concerto. My mother's wish was fulfilled, but her absence felt even more painful. I kept expecting to see her next to my father in the front row. But he looked happy and proud and at that moment I sensed her presence and played for her. After the tour, I had to break the news to my father that my marriage was also dead. It was the only time I felt grateful that my mother was not alive. She would have been devastated and even more upset and worried than I was, while my father's matter of fact reaction was reassuringly optimistic: 'Oh well, it can't be helped,' he said, 'you've managed to overcome so many obstacles before, you will make it through this one as well.' There was another tearful departure at the airport before I went back to my broken life and uncertain future. Years of pain and suffering followed. It was so awful that I have wiped most of it from my memory. The hardest thing was to see my children upset and unhappy. For years they did not want to see their father and I was left to care for them on my own and for sure, made many mistakes. Those years seemed like a never-ending earthquake demolishing the foundations of everything I had. I lost my mother, my marriage, my music festival, my confidence. Even my dear analyst had gone back to Zurich. I drifted for four years, lost and frightened through these ruins, before the divorce was finalised. I had lived with the illusion that once the divorce was over, I would be relieved and free to start a new life, but what happened was exactly the opposite. I collapsed, not able to blame anybody, slowly and painfully becoming aware of the part I had played. The picture wasn't pleasant. I was equally guilty in creating the problems between us, demanding without being aware of John's limits and needs. I had disregarded my own limits and had imposed my views of life on him. While concentrating on his faults, I had remained blind to my own, and now they piled up in front of me about to devour me. The road to self-realisation is long and winding. There are sudden periods of illumination followed by darkness. I would take a few steps forward, hopeful and strong, then fall into a deep despair, as if paralysed. But strangely enough, I had the sense I was not alone. One afternoon, I reached my lowest point. Lying on the sofa, unable to move, I stared blindly at the ceiling, when suddenly I felt an invisible hand holding mine. I began to see the hazy contour of a face in profile above me. It seemed made of light. My eyes followed the image. It grew bigger, extending out across the ceiling, then bigger still, growing beyond the house and into space. The light increased and the face turned to me – it was my own face looking down with a smile. At that moment everything changed. The vision of that smile has never left me. Slowly, I stood up. I was on the way home.

And so began my second life; almost thirty years of inner and outer travel, discovery, wonder and also times of despair. I came to understand that suffering and failure doesn't mean being wrong or unfortunate, rather it is a necessary part of life's journey. I had many new encounters, sudden profound realisations, read widely and attended different courses. Inevitably, I made wrong turnings and it took me a long time to release the deeply rooted identities to which I had clung. Growing happens in stages and more by failing than by succeeding. Walking in a dark mood along Piccadilly, one rainy November day, I glanced absent-mindedly in the window of a bookshop, when the title of a book drew my attention: 'Ruins of the Heart'. That spoke to me. I went inside and the book was on a table straight in front of me. I opened it at random. A long poem. Oh, I hate long poems, especially in English, not my mother tongue. I flicked through the pages – all long poems. I wanted to put the book down, but it wouldn't let me, it stuck to my hand. I moved to a brighter spot and began to read. Bit by bit, the poems melted my resistance and touched me deeply. I bought the book and sat in a café next door, reading from cover to cover. The more I read, the more I loved it. It was Jelaludin Rumi. I took him home for good. Before long, I had acquired every available translation of his poetry. Rumi became my companion, my teacher, my inspiration and love. He sustained me through the difficult years of change and does so to this day. He is the driving force of all my actions. His poems inspired me to give many concerts, marrying his words with music. They have also inspired my paintings and led me to publish books of his work in collaboration with a Persian friend. The spark that Rumi ignited lit up my world. I kept feeling that I had met him before, he was so familiar. Then, to my amazement, I came across a little tattered book I had bought when I first came to England, attracted by the beautiful cypress tree on its cover and because the stories and quotations were short, perfect for a beginner in English. They gave me comfort and later I read them to my children as they were growing up. The name of the author had remained invisible to me until now. How miraculous to find that Rumi had been there all along. One particular line of his, *'Close the door of words and open love's window'*… unlocked my heart and let sunlight penetrate my stony prison, my own Iron Curtain.

I was free to go where I didn't dare dream. The forbidden world I longed for as a little girl, fishing with my father at the tiny seaport in Bulgaria, was now calling me to open my wings and fly even though these wings were damaged. I was still lacking courage, and often counted my losses, looking backwards instead of ahead. It took many years of travel to repair my wings. Each journey mended and straightened a feather – India, the inspiration, Morocco, the strength, Greece, the shimmer of blue. In the high desert of New Mexico, I found a beloved sister and wrote the first words of this book. All these places were precious gifts that added power to my wings, expanded my horizons and enriched my life.

The greatest of these journeys were the deserts. For seven years I spent two-week silent retreats in the Sinai and Sahara. I rode camels, lived simply with the Bedouins and slept under the stars. Here, I met nature in its raw power, a landscape of constant change and shifting sands, hardly touched by humans, mighty and pure. This is the only place on earth where I have felt God's presence. Even now, I can still sense the sand under my feet – cold as snow in the morning, burning at noon, and delightfully silky at night. Walking in this vast nothingness, hearing your heartbeat drumming in your temples, see-sawing between the sun and the moon, you meet your Self. Once I sat under a palm tree and watched a beetle drawing lacy patterns in the sand. Being part of this profound silence and beauty – burning, empty, fierce – was ecstasy. Exiled from the little me, I found great freedom. But I wouldn't have known what freedom meant without having known captivity.

The moment you step on the desert sand, you enter another world. The sun at noon, like an enraged lion, devours everything and stops everybody in their tracks. The Bedouins, kings of the desert, agile and slender in their long jellabas, move so effortlessly and so elegantly that it seems you are watching some ancient ritual dance. In the cool of evening, they appear and disappear, tending the fire, making bread, brewing pots of tea. The silhouettes of their camels against the night sky are noble and imposing. In the bitter-cold nights the bright stars look so close you can almost touch them. Under their gaze, sleep is sweet. The eyes relax in the emptiness, the ears in the resounding silence. Words cannot define this beauty. The desert is a living poem.

There are no signposts in the desert, caravans are guided by the stars.
In the darkness of despair, hope is the only light.

Rumi

The Sahara

News travels slowly in the desert –
camels cruise over the dunes with
elegant deliberation. You gaze at
the emptiness, immense and silent –
so silent, you hear your heartbeat.
You listen. Sighs, murmurs, held
for ages in the sand, the footsteps
of pilgrims, the Desert Fathers,
the breath of prophets before their
words were imprisoned in the pages
of the Holy Books.

In Sahara's translucent sky
I spin past galaxies, among
billions of stars. Sometimes,
I am a ring around Saturn
revolving particles of ice and dust.
Sometimes, soft moonlight
bending over earth.
Here, solitude is mysterious
and terrifying. Thoughts dissolve
in the immensity of silence.

Sinai

The desert sky wears many robes –
tender pink at dawn, silky blue
in the morning, flaming red at sunset.
The scorching white of noon strangles
all colours. The rocks are hot,
the sand is hot, the sky weighs a ton.

We wait, under the Bedouin's shade
cooked in a vast oven. An hour
becomes a month. We are guests
of a desert that devours its guests.
Slowly the sun loosens its grip.
Colours – mauve, cadmium, azure
appear in the rock's crevices.

Bedouins spring to action, hoarse cries
of the camels signal departure.
The air is cooler on the camel's back.
You glide between sky and sand
rocked by the hypnotic rhythm.
With nothing to lean on
the spirit rises.

Beyond Limits

Sahara sand is as soft as flour spilt
from heaven, piled into dunes, edges
flying off, like strands of hair in the wind.
Spread across the sky, angel wings
hang motionless: feathers of
delicate pink over transparent blue,
echoed in the sand at my feet.

I am an intruder caught in the middle
of a sacred conversation, not knowing
am I on sand, in the sky or under the sea?
There is no boundary. The desert breathes,
swells into human shapes
like waves, rising and falling.

I walk over dead bodies,
layer upon layer all the way
to the core of the earth.
I strain my ears – murmurs, sighs,
words, rise from under my feet.
Worlds into endless worlds.

Acknowledgements

My warmest thanks to Mirabai Starr without whose encouragement and support this book would never have come into being. Thanks also for the helpful advice and suggestions from friends and colleagues in my writing group. I am grateful to Sarah Cheesbrough who has brought old, faded photographs back to life and especially so to Gina Cowen for her fine firm editing and great sense of humour.